Northwest Outdoor Vacation Guide

by Ira Spring
and Harvey Manning

The Writing Works
A division of Morse Press
Seattle, WA

Published by The Writing Works
Division of Morse Press, Inc.
417 East Pine Street
Seattle, WA 98122

Library of Congress Catalog Number: 81-52031
ISBN: 0-916076-44-X

CONTENTS

PREFACE

We had two reasons for writing this book.

First was the advent (on the horizon, if not quite here yet) of $2-a-gallon gasoline. As visitation figures of national parks show, more and more people are driving less and less. The old-style vacation, burning up 2000 miles of highway a week, pausing only to click the camera at postcard scenes and pick up the decals, is going out of favor.

Coming in is the vacation that doesn't cover seven states and all the national parks of the West on one swing but settles down to "mine" the attractions of a smaller area. To us this is far more enjoyable. For example, the whole Oregon coast can be driven in a day or two, and a lovely drive it is. But how much lovelier to spend weeks on the coast, taking leisurely time to explore picturesque beaches, peer into tidal pools, hike forest trails, fish the high seas, ride a jet boat up the Rogue River, swim and sun, or just laze around while the kids slide down a sand dune. Weeks won't be enough. You'll go home sorry you didn't have months.

Or, think about a vacation that doesn't start by putting a thousand miles of highway behind the family car but is based in a nearby city—maybe the one you live in. For example, Seattle. Ride the ferries, tour mountain highways, rent a canoe and paddle in the Arboretum, bicycle the Burke-Gilman Trail on a rented bike, float a river in a rubber raft, even climb Mt. Rainier with a guide. Do the things visitors do but residents often shun. There's so much to do you might not even find time to eat fish and chips on the waterfront or take the elevator to the top of the Space Needle or walk the Underground City of the Skid Road.

We've selected 18 vacations that sample the Northwest with activities to tempt the whole family—different families—and keep everybody busy for a week or two or three. So you can't get to the Grand Canyon or the Alps this year —try the Olympic Peninsula, the High Desert of Oregon, the West Coast of Vancouver Island, the Idaho Panhandle. You may forget you ever considered any other choice.

The second reason we wrote the book was to emphasize self-propelled activities in the out-of-doors. Virtually every large city has a good guidebook to

Toleak Point, Olympic National Park, Washington

the local scene, and every chamber of commerce gladly will fill your satchel with brochures on places to stay and things to do, usually those that cost money. We mention some of this but mainly to refer the reader to other sources who know the subject better. We try to tell what the chambers of commerce usually don't — where to take a hike or watch a bird.

A caution about self-propelled sports of the thrills-and-chills species: The Northwest is a land of mountains that stir the ambition, and a person of imagination may suppose that if he buys an ice ax he can go anywhere. We say little here about climbing. The trained mountaineer already knows where he wants to go. The inexperienced had better get some training. Consequently, the only climbing we mention here is with professional guides.

Similarly with river-rafting. In recent years white-water rafting has grown as popular as climbing. We assume that if you own a raft you know the sport and where to gain expert information about rivers. We've not dwelt on danger because no reputable firm will rent a raft to an inexperienced person except for short floats on very smooth water. Again we stress the need for the beginner to sign up with a reliable guide. The U.S. Forest Service supplies lists of licensed guides for various rivers of the Northwest.

In conclusion, let me say we by no means discourage coming great distances to enjoy the Northwest. The vacations in this book certainly will be as much enjoyed by the family that flies in from New Jersey as the family that lives in Portland. However, driving thousands of miles on highways is the kind of fun that most folks get tired of in a hurry. In our opinion, once you reach the chosen scene you have a better time if you concentrate on doing a lot in a little space rather than a little over a lot. It also cuts way down on the gas bill.

IRA SPRING
HARVEY MANNING

VANCOUVER ISLAND

British Columbia

Hub of the Wheel Vacation

Pacific Ocean on one side, Strait of Georgia on the other, wilderness mountains in the center, and a very English-like city on the south end, Vancouver Island has vacations for folks who like to tour rose gardens and eat fancy meals in a grand hotel, folks who like to walk beaches and alpine meadows, and folks who simply like to roam about in boats.

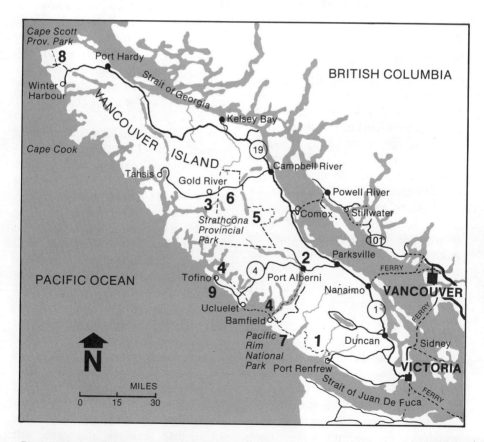

Boat harbor at Tofino

Provincial Parliament Building in Victoria

Where to Stay

More will be said about accommodations in following sections but a first decision is—where to put the hub? Victoria has fine hotels and excellent restaurants and plenty of nearby activities to fill your days. Elsewhere on the island, wherever one might want to base oneself, there's always a handy motel or campground.

Our personal choice of headquarters is in or near Nanaimo, an easy day's drive from most island attractions. Nanaimo has a good hotel, a number of motels, and camping at Ivy Green Provincial Park, just north of Ladysmith.

Victoria

Personally I dislike big cities—too busy, too noisy, too many people, too much concrete that makes my feet ache for soft forest trails. Victoria is no exception. Nevertheless, the wonders of the place make the blisters worth it.

At one end of the spectrum of accommodations is the commercial campground near Fort Victoria, from which you can ride a city bus into town. At the other end is the historic Empress Hotel, most prestigious in the Northwest, famed for turning away Bing Crosby because he wasn't wearing a tie.

The city offers a wealth of interesting drives and scenic vistas, city parks and amusement park and five golf courses, Sea Land with a killer whale that loves to perform, Maritime Museum, sailboat rides ranging from two hours to a five-day school, windsurfing, swimming, harbor cruises, castles, even a reproduction of Ann Hathaway's cottage. A chamber of commerce brochure leads to these and other interesting directions.

Many a visitor comes to Victoria specifically and entirely for Butchart Gardens and spends every day here. (They're just as beautiful at night.)

We recommend an introductory "short" walk of only eight blocks — that may well take you all day. Start from the center of the city, parking along Wharf Street or close. Afoot, begin on the broad sidewalk along Government Street, overlooking the Inner Harbor. Pass the Empress Hotel (peek in the lobby) and the Wax Museum (go in) to the Tally-Ho stands; perhaps take a ride around town on the Tally-Ho. Next is the Undersea Garden with more than 5000 marine creatures. Cross the park-like grounds of the Parliament Building (this is the capital city of British Columbia), over Government Street, to the Provincial Museum.

Stop. We went in for a quick 15-minute look-see and came out starry-eyed three hours later, frustrated we couldn't stay longer. The museum is bursting at the seams with history, both natural and human, particularly emphasizing Indian culture.

From there enter Thunderbird Park, featuring an Indian longhouse and a collection of totem poles. Return to the starting point by way of Douglas Street, visiting the Classic Car Museum and Miniature World.

The Island Highway and Sidetrips

In the 300 miles from Victoria to the end of the pavement at Port Hardy, the Island Highway, marked Canada 1 to Nanaimo, then B.C. Road 19, traverses some of the best marine scenery in British Columbia— which means in North America. An early climax is Malahat Drive, where the highway climbs a 1000-foot bluff to a breathtaking vista over Saanich Inlet to Sidney. Water views are few for a while, but from Parksville to Campbell River the way repeatedly touches the Strait of Georgia. The road then goes

inland, where wilderness closes in, unmarked by civilization. A swing to water again, at Kelsey Bay, is followed by more inland wildland, then Port McNeill and the highway end at Port Hardy.

The highway is swell but the sidetrips are terrific. Some are on paved roads, others on gravel, good to poor to adventurous. There are miles of logging roads—Vancouver Island is becoming one big clearcut. At certain times, well-marked on signs, these roads are open to public travel; for an infinity of explorations buy the two-volume guidebook *Logging Road Travel.*

The first sidetrip is from Victoria, following B.C. Road 14 along the Strait of Juan de Fuca, with views over the water to the Olympic Mountains, to road's end at Port Renfrew, southern end of the Shipwreck Trail (see below).

The highlight of the trip is a natural museum of marine life. From behind the "pub" (you can't miss it) drive a rough dirt road until it becomes

Butchart Gardens in Victoria

too rough, then walk about 2½ miles to a large flat rock, exposed at low tide. Find an easy way onto the rock and see the creatures living in small potholes eroded by gravel swirled around by the surf.

The next sidetrip is from Duncan, home of the famous handknit Cowichan Indian sweater, no two of the same design, to Lake Cowichan for the fishing.

Next, from Parksville, north of Nanaimo, drive B.C. Highway 4 west to Port Alberni and a fork in the road. The right fork, paved, leads to the Long Beach section of Pacific Rim National Park, and the left, dirt, goes to Bamfield, northern terminus of the Shipwreck Trail. Both are described below.

From Campbell River paved road B.C. 28 goes to the town of Gold River and Muchalat Inlet, where a dirt road continues to the town of Tahsis, on the way passing Strathcona Park Lodge.

From between Port McNeill and Port Hardy a paved road goes to Port Alice on Neroutsos Inlet.

From Port Hardy a dirt road leads to Winter Harbor on Quatsino Sound, near the northern tip of Vancouver Island. End of the line. Except you can walk a trail to Cape Scott, the absolute end. Or take the ferry to Prince Rupert and on to the Queen Charlotte Islands.

Fishing

Vancouver Island is a few years behind the mainland in getting "civilized," and fishing there is of the sort that used to be found everywhere in the Northwest. Streams and lakes are loaded with trout; the salt water perhaps has no more salmon than that off the Washington coast, but it has a lot fewer fishermen.

Just about every dock along the Island Highway has charter boats taking customers out in the Strait of Georgia; some marinas rent small boats so you can do it yourself.

Deserving special mention is **Mitlenatch Island Provincial Park,** a small island in the northern reaches of the Strait of Georgia, reached from

Cowichan sweaters in a store at Duncan

The Bastion in Nanaimo, built in 1853 by the Hudson Bay Company

Campbell River via charter boat or rental boat. Going and coming, cast your line. If there in May or June, walk the sea meadows amid famous display of the wildflowers. From a polite distance, so as not to disturb, observe nesting gulls, oyster catchers, and pigeon guillemots.

For the ocean, three firms in Ucluelet and one in Tofino offer deep-sea fishing.

Water Touring

Yes, it's an island, so you don't get on without a ferry ride—over the Strait of Juan de Fuca from Port Angeles, or farther south from Seattle, through the San Juan Islands from Anacortes (reservation needed), or over the Strait of Georgia from Tsawwassen or Horseshoe Bay, both near Vancouver, or from the Sunshine Coast, or north from Prince Rupert. These are the most exciting car-ferry voyages in Northwest waters, and many a person comes just to ride the ferries—with or without a car (the latter is much cheaper). However, there are other trips on littler boats.

Most famous of vessels is the *Lady Rose,* which since 1937 has carried freight and passengers through Barkley Sound. Though Bamfield and Ucluelet, the towns for which it once was the sole regular connection to "outside," now are reached by roads, in between are miles of wilderness forest and mountains in Pacific Rim National Park. Trips leave Port Alberni daily at 8 a.m., going on alternate days to Bamfield and Ucluelet, stopping en route at remote villages and passing through the Broken Group Islands. The capacity is 100 passengers; during summer, when tourists outnumber local citizens, it's best to sign up early.

Based at Gold River, the

Steam train at the British Columbia Forest Museum near Duncan

Uchuck III cruises the West Coast, with views to the mountains and to Nootka Sound, little changed since Captain Cook sailed by more than 200 years ago.

The three boat companies in Ucluelet take passengers out among the Broken Group Islands; the one in Tofino, to Hot Springs Cove and Sea Lion Rocks.

Tired of the sound of motors? Rather be sailing? Viking Charters, Nanaimo, offers seven-hour cruises aboard a 41-foot ketch.

Canoeing

Vancouver Island is the ultimate of all saltwater touring areas among experienced kayakers and canoeists. "Experienced" must be stressed—even the lee side of the island can whip up furious seas, and the ocean side is—well, it's the shipwreck side.

The Gulf Islands are best for the less experienced; especially in calm weather there are many lovely short paddles to and around and between and among uninhabited islets. For this area you'll need to bring your own craft.

Canoes can be rented from S.S.S. Charters, in Ucluelet, opening a world of watery wonders. In good weather you can safely paddle to the Broken Group Islands; Toquart Bay is

closer to the islands and more protected, a better put-in and take-out. Towards Tofino is Grice Bay, very protected; however, when the tide goes out, it goes out forever, and the unwary boater can be stuck in mudflats up to six hours waiting for high tide. With a camping permit from B.C. Forest Service, overnight trips can be made to the head of Tofino Inlet. The other direction, out to Tofino, is through a narrow channel where tides and winds can churn horrible waves; watch it.

Hiking

For all that it is a vast (former) wilderness, trails are comparatively few on Vancouver Island. The B.C. Forest Service never has taken more than scant notice of recreation as a forest use. The logging industry "owns" the woods, and most of what trails once existed have become haul roads. The island nevertheless has a mountain wilderness, a place of snows and flowers. Most notably it has a beach wilderness, perhaps the grandest in the Northwest.

In addition to the hikes mentioned here, others are discussed in following sections.

Strathcona Provincial Park. The Vancouver Island Mountains rise to a climax of 7219 feet in Mt. Golden Hinde, center of the wilderness core of Strathcona Provincial Park. The best introduction is the Forbidden Plateau. From Courtenay drive to the Forbidden Plateau Ski Resort and find the trail, climbing 2500 feet in 3 miles to the edge of the plateau. Explore alpine lakes and heather gardens. Gaze to four other mountain ranges in two nations.

A base for more hiking in mountains and on beaches—and for canoeing, kayaking, sailing, climbing, and anthropological studies—is the

Cathedral Grove Provincial Park near Port Alberni

Strathcona Park Lodge and Outdoor Education Center. You can simply relax or fish at the lodge, located in forests between Buttle Lake and Upper Campbell Lake, reached by driving Gold River Road 20 miles from Campbell River. However, most visitors participate in one or more of the 40 different outdoor programs. Expert instructors give instruction and lead trips. For a brochure write the lodge, P.O. Box 2160, Campbell River, B.C. V9W 5C9, or radiophone through the telephone operator at Campbell River.

Shipwreck Trail. Over the generations and centuries ship after ship—at least 60—piled up on the stormy West Coast of Vancouver Island, and the wild sea swallowed up many a brave sailor man. More tragically, many who escaped the sea were then swallowed up by the wild woods.

In 1909, therefore, a 50-mile trail was built from Bamfield to Port Renfrew so mariners could escape the wilderness. Called the Shipwreck Trail, or Lifesaving Trail, it fell into disuse with development of modern rescue methods. Then, after the "wilderness beach" of Olympic National Park had become super-popular and super-crowded, hikers seeking solitude and adventure began prowling the island shore. Now included in Pacific Rim National Park, in a few short years the trail has grown to be only less popular than the Olympic beach.

But it's rougher. To do the entire 50 miles requires five to 10 days, including a crossing of the Nitinat River by Indian canoe, bridges high over gorges that are *not* recommended for the person who suffers from vertigo, and stretches of mean and nasty

Strathcona Park Lodge guests kayaking on Campbell River

Fish dock at Tofino

brush and mud. However, the trail can be easily and pleasantly sampled on day hikes from both ends; get a map from the National Park Service and consult the guidebook, *West Coast Trail*.

Cape Scott Provincial Park. The north tip calls the imagination. From Port Hardy drive forest roads 30 miles, passing Holberg, to the start of a trail that goes 18 miles through woods, by abandoned homesteads, to sandy beaches broken by rocky headlands where seals and sea lions sun and whales can be seen swimming from Alaska to California and back.

Bicycling

Victoria, when I first was there years ago, was so very very English that retired British military men dressed in tweed jackets and caps and knickers, smoking pipes, pedaled about town on bicycles as if there was nothing at all ridiculous about it. Of course, they were right, and nowadays thousands of folks bicycle around Victoria on city streets and quiet back roads. Rentals are available at agencies noted in the Yellow Pages.

The Island Highway and the paved sideroads are popular for long-distance, camping-out bicycle trips, though on some stretches the cars blaze by and shoulders are narrow to zero.

Our notion of bicycling heaven is the Gulf Islands, where roads are lonesome, the sun shines, and the living is easy. Park on the other side of the water and take your bike on the ferry for a day's tour of any of the five islands that have ferry service. Or take your overnight gear and bike them all.

Gulf Islands

Some people spend their entire vacations on one of the many islands in the Gulf (or Strait) of Georgia Islands, also known as the Canadian San Juans. In the rainshadow of two mountain ranges the summers are dry, the fishing is good, and resorts and campgrounds provide comfortable bases.

Galiano, Mayne, Saturna, the Penders, and Saltspring Islands are on B.C. Ferry runs. For other islands you'll need to bring your own boat or rent one from a marina.

Pacific Rim National Park

In 1970 the federal government of Canada recognized that the West Coast of Vancouver Island was as wild and scenic a stretch of beaches and bays as any in the world so close to so many people. The park extends 75 miles along the coast from Port Renfrew to Tofino, in three segments. Part of the park has roadside beaches. Part is as wild as when poor sailors were washed ashore and succumbed to starvation or lonesomeness or were just plain rained to death.

For a hiker the Shipwreck Trail is the essence of the park. For less strenuous or simply different introductions the Long Beach area is excellent with its wide, sandy beaches, 9 miles long, easy trails, canoeing, two picturesque fishing villages, and some of the best fishing in the West are the drawing cards.

Motels and commercial campgrounds are on the beach at Ucluelet and towards Tofino. The park has a limited number of car-camping sites, well back from the beach, and a walk-in (½ mile) camp on the beach at Schooner Cove.

To get there, turn west from Parksville on B.C. Highway 4 to Port Alberni and follow signs to Tofino and Ucluelet. The road is paved but slow going, what with twists and turns and steep hills; take note there is no gas in the 60 miles from Alberni to Ucluelet. The drive is a beauty, passing a series of deep lakes in glacier-carved troughs and glimpses of snowy peaks. Halfway to Alberni the highway goes through Cathedral Grove, trees between 300 and 800 years old. Port Alberni has large sawmills and pulpmills that wel-

Shore birds at Long Beach

come visitors; check with the local tourist information office.

Within sound but not sight of the ocean, Highway 4 forks. The left is to Ucluelet, but first go right to the Long Beach Unit of Pacific Rim Park. Stop at the visitor center for maps and then proceed to the beach. Views from the road are blocked by trees, so park and walk the few feet to the sand and then walk, swim, sunbathe, clam, or sit and look. Afterward tour Tofino and Ucluelet, fishing villages that in season are humming with boats unloading catches; Tofino is our favorite. Be sure to have plenty of film for your camera. Allow time for fishing, canoeing, boat rides, or whatever is your pleasure.

Don't forget the *hiking*. Between Ucluelet and Tofino there once was a corduroy road, cedar planks laid in the muck so wagons and horses and people wouldn't sink out of sight. Parts of the Wickaninnish and Willowbrae Trails follow remnants of the corduroy.

The trails, through forests to beaches, are 1½ and 1 mile long.

In the Long Beach Unit are seven short trails. One is a short loop in a rain forest. The other six, ½ to 1½ miles long, go to the beach. One beach path, the Gold Mine Trail, passes old mine dumps and remains of a dredge used in the early 1900s to sift gold from the sands.

Broken Group Islands. In the mouth of Barkley Sound is a group of more than 100 islands, arguably the best part of the park. The only way there is, obviously, by boat. The *Lady Rose* winds through en route to Ucluelet and will let you off on Gibraltar Island. Charter boats based in Ucluelet also take passengers on tour. However, the best explorations are on your own, by motor or canoe. Both can be rented in Ucluelet. You'll need nautical charts for navigation and the Park Service map showing approved camps as well as springs—but carry drinking water in case these are dry.

Ferry between Horseshoe Bay and Nanaimo

Tourist Information

Greater Victoria Visitors Center, 1117 Wharf Street, Victoria, B.C., (604) 387-6417

Bicycle rental:

Oak Bay Bicycle, 1968 Oak Bay, Victoria, B.C., (604) 598-4111

Hiking:

Brochures

Ministry of Lands, Parks and Housing, Parks & Outdoor Recreation Division, Parliament Buildings, Victoria, B.C. V8V 1X4

Maps

Surveys and Mapping Branch, Ministry of Environment, Parliament Buildings, Victoria, B.C. V8V 1X4

Outdoor Activities

For information on Canadian Mountain Guides, Bicycling Association, B.C. Camping Association, River Outfitters Association of B.C., and activities such as skydiving, hang-gliding, river rafting, etc.

Outdoor Recreation Council of B.C., 1200 Hornby Street, Vancouver, B.C. V6Z 2E2, (604) 687-3333

Outdoor Education Centre, Strathcona Park Lodge, Box 2160, Campbell River, B.C. V9W 5C9

Phone: Call Area Code 604. Ask for Campbell River radio operator and then ask for Strathcona Lodge JL93546

Reference Books

The Victoria Guidebook, by Betty Campbell, Campbell's Publishing, Ltd., 201-1150 Rockland Ave., Victoria, B.C. V8V 3H7

Victoria in Your Pocket, Trivco Distributors, Ltd., (address unknown)

Victoria on Foot–Walking Tours of Victoria's Old Town, (book on historical buildings), Terrapin Publishing, Ltd., (address unknown)

Kids, Kids, Kids on Vancouver Island, by Betty Campbell & Daniel Woods, Saltaire Publishing Co., P.O. Box 2003, Sidney, B.C. V8L 3S3

The West Coast Trail, Sierra Club of B.C., Box 385, West Vancouver, B.C.

Logging Road Travel, Vols. 1 & 2, by Alec & Taffy Merriman, Saltaire Publishing Co.

Hiking Trails, Vols. I II & III, by Outdoor Club of Victoria, P.O. Box 1875, Victoria, B.C. V8W 2Y3

103 Hikes in Southwestern British Columbia, by David Macaree, The Mountaineers, 719 Pike St., Seattle, WA 98101

Golf Courses in Victoria

Cedar Hill Golf Course	Uplands Golf Club
Gorge Vale Golf Course	Victoria Golf Club

VANCOUVER

British Columbia

Hub of the Wheel Vacation

Actually, to call this a single vacation is to flagrantly misrepresent the facts and undervalue the attractions. Vancouver itself is one vacation—no other city of North America offers such a wealth of magnificent scenery and outdoor fun within its limits. Close to the east are the valley, then the canyon, of the Fraser River, and the mountains of E.C. Manning Provincial Park—two or three more vacations. At least another lies to the north in the alpine meadows of Garibaldi Provincial Park and still another on the Sun-

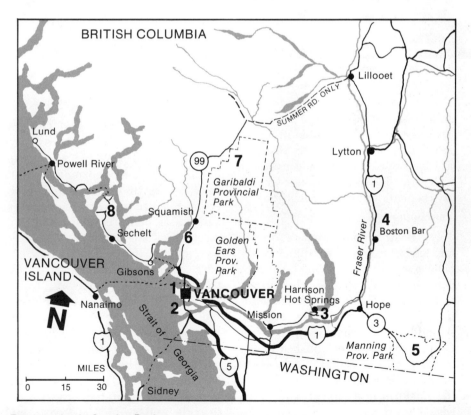

Totem poles in Stanley Park

Lions Gate Bridge across Burrard Inlet

shine Coast. Finally, there are nearly as many vacations possible in winter as in summer. Nevertheless, all can be at least sampled from Vancouver as a hub. If you have enough time, you can try them all. Like, say, a lifetime.

Vancouver

Boating and fishing on salt water, hiking miles of woodland trails, believe it or not, and *skiing,* all can be done *in the city.* Among other attractions are a wildlife refuge, planetarium, gardens, skyscrapers, and the second-largest Chinatown on the West Coast. Base can be established in any of the dozens of deluxe hotels downtown and on English Bay, a motel on the outskirts, or a campground on the edge of town.

Stanley Park and Others. Dedicated in 1889 when there wasn't much city and parkland was cheap, Stanley Park is enormous — 1000 acres on the tip of the peninsula between Burrard Inlet and English Bay, salt water on three sides and skyscrapers on the other. It's on everybody's list of the world's greatest city parks. Man has added much to the park — miniature railway, totem poles, playgrounds, gardens, children's zoo, aquarium, picnic grounds, tea house, pitch-and-putt golf, swimming pools, tennis courts, shuffleboard, lawn bowling, lighthouse, Lord Stanley Monument, Nine O'clock Gun. But the park is nature-centered — the beaches to walk and swim, the forests and meadows with miles of hiking trails (walking around the park perimeter is 6 miles) and bicycle trails and fitness trails—and a new roller-skating trail. The park is home to ducks, Canadian geese, and swans; when the tide is out, dozens of great blue herons feed in shallow waters, nonchalant about people walking close by.

Stanley Park does not stand alone. Virtually the entire waterfront of English Bay is a park with wide, sandy beaches superb for swimming and walking.

Across the Lions Gate Bridge is Lighthouse Park, 185 acres of virgin forest laced with trails. An interpretive center specializes in explaining nature to children. There also is a lighthouse.

For walks in all these parks and elsewhere in the lowlands, see *Easy Hiking Around Vancouver.*

Great blue heron at Stanley Park is undisturbed by people

Bicycling in Stanley Park

Chinatown section of Vancouver

Downtown History. The harbor tours based at Stanley Park are excellent for a water perspective on the bays and estuaries that soon after the first settlement in 1865 began drawing the marine traffic that was to make Vancouver a world port.

For a land perspective, walk back in time along streets of old Gastown, on the waterfront, and sit at a sidewalk cafe in Maple Tree Square. Then walk the other way to Chinatown.

Because of the Empire (now Commonwealth) connection, and the fact that during all the years the United States was at Cold War with half the world the ships of the Soviet Union and the People's Republic of China routinely called here, Vancouver has more of a feeling of belonging to the world than any other city on the West Coast of North America.

Steveston. This quiet fishing village at the mouth of the Fraser River once was distant from Vancouver. It hasn't moved, but Vancouver has and now nearly engulfs the old village. However, changes have been slow here and the past lives. On

Gastown section of Vancouver

weekends fishermen tie up at the dock and sell their catches right off the decks of their boats.

Drive south on B.C. Highway 99. Just before the Fraser River tunnel turn west on Steveston Road.

Lower Fraser River

Among rivers of the West the Fraser is second in size only to the Columbia and in scenery is unsurpassed. Nearing the coast the great surge of waters from several mountain ranges meanders over a broad floodplain, green-squared with lush farms, from which the Cascade Range on one side and the British Columbia Coast Range on the other leap thousands of feet to snowy summits. This sub-vacation begins from the hub of Vancouver with a 70-mile drive east on Highway 1, the Trans-Canada Highway, past Chilliwack to the Agassiz-Harrison Hot Springs junction.

The sideroad leads to the town of Harrison Hot Springs, best-known for the heavily-advertised hotel that has its own hot-spring swimming pool, golf course, tennis courts, and fine foods served in the grand manner. It's very much a dress-up place, for dinner at least. The town, definitely camper-casual, has a public hot-spring swimming pool, numerous motels, restaurants, and commercial campgrounds; another campground is in nearby Sasquatch Provincial Park.

Small lakes in the vicinity are said by the chamber of commerce to be teeming with trout—rainbow, cutthroat, and Dolly Varden. The champion of waterways is Harrison Lake, 45 miles long, an inland fjord curving far north into a mountain wilderness. The town has a beautiful sandy beach on the lake. Canoes can be rented for local paddling—and bicycles, too, for pedaling around to gain fresh perspec-

Selling fish at Steveston

tives on water and peaks. To see more, take an excursion on the tour boat.

Fraser Canyon

Upstream from the broad floodplain is the narrow canyon, a V-gash in the Coast Range through which the Fraser flows from the arid interior, the Caribou Country. Tours can be based at motels in Hope, Yale, and Lytton, or at campgrounds.

Highway vistas are airy and impressive enough, but the views from cablecars above the river are dizzying. At Boston Bar, 40 miles east of Hope, an automobile ferry takes one vehicle at a time. If you're planning to use this

service, we advise you not to watch a crossing until after you've made your own—it looks very hairy, that tiny platform dangling from a thin cable. The Swiss-built Air-Tram at Hell's Gate, passengers only, looks sturdier —reassuring, considering the horrid turmoil of the river as it churns through the gate of Hell. On the far side are the fish ladder climbed by 2,000,000 salmon a year, interpretive displays, movies, gift shops, and a restaurant.

To really know the Fraser, float it. The chamber of commerce lists three firms offering raft trips. Among them is Whitewater Adventures, Ltd., 105 West 6th Ave., Vancouver, B.C. V5Y 1K3, phone (604) 879-6701. Trips on the Fraser and Thompson Rivers last a day or longer.

E.C. Manning Provincial Park

In the Cascades on the American side of the border are North Cascades National Park and Pasayten Wilderness. On the Canadian side is E.C. Manning Provincial Park, a place to roam alpine meadows or paddle a canoe. To reach the park, drive Trans-Canada Highway 1 east from Vancouver 80 miles to Hope, then 40 more miles on B.C. Highway 3. Hope has motels and a commercial campground. Near park headquarters is a modern motel. In the park are campgrounds.

Lightning Lake, near park headquarters, is lovely to look at, delightful to canoe because it's closed to motorboats. Rentals are available from the concessionaire. The swimming and picnicking are also fun, and nearby trails lead into forests—nice walking.

Lightning Lake, Manning Park

Garibaldi Lake and Mt. Garibaldi

The best introduction to highland hiking is the Heather Trail. From park headquarters drive the Blackwall Peak Road to its end at an elevation of 6867 feet. Views begin from the car and continue on the trail, which in season is a dozen colors of alpine flowers. Spend a half-day or three days; for overnight trips a camping permit is required. Another popular hike is a three-day loop over the border into the Pasayten Wilderness.

Garibaldi Provincial Park

The British Columbia Coast Range begins literally within the city limits of Vancouver, rising in steep forests and granite cliffs thousands of feet from salt water. To the north the coast is cut by a succession of glacier-carved fjords that rival in grandeur those of Norway. The first is Howe Sound, route to another natural wonder—Mount Garibaldi, an 8787-foot volcano, centerpiece of Garibaldi Provincial Park.

Getting there is half the fun. Drive from North Vancouver and Horseshoe Bay on B.C. Highway 99, blasted from cliffs that plunge into Howe Sound, with new views of fjords and mountains around every corner.

Stop at Britannia Beach to visit the British Columbia Museum of Mining, featuring a ride on a mining train deep inside a mountain to the compressors and drills miners used to dig the hole. We know of no other mine tour like this in the Northwest.

Continue to Squamish, a village bounded on one side by the head of Howe Sound, on all others by mountains.

Now back up the 42 miles to Vancouver and consider an alternative mode of travel. Park your car in North Vancouver, near the railroad station, and take the *Royal Hudson,* a

Ferry on Howe Sound

steam locomotive that pulls a train up Howe Sound, along that same water-and-mountain route, to Squamish — a splendid way to spend a day. However, passenger service continues on this line through the mountains to Caribou Country and onward to salt water at Prince George; get the schedule from B.C. Railways and invent a whole new vacation, car-free.

From Squamish onward motels and campgrounds are plentiful. Whistler, a year-around resort on the edge of Garibaldi Park, has hotels, condominiums, swimming pool, golf, and a gondola ride high on Whistler Mountain to summer snowfields and glorious views of glaciered peaks of the Coast Range.

Paved highway continues to Pemberton. From there a forest road continues to Lillooet but is not recommended for ordinary passenger cars. However, those that make it can do a loop trip back down the Fraser Canyon.

Because the B.C. Forest Service doesn't officially recognize the existence of hikers, good trails are few in the province. Most are in provincial parks, and Garibaldi has the best. The favorite is the trail that climbs 2500 feet in 4 miles to 4500-foot Garibaldi Lake. The way continues 1½ miles in parkland and flowers and alpine vistas to Black Tusk Meadows, 5500 feet. Black Tusk and the peak of Garibaldi are weirdly different from volcanoes of the Cascades to the south. Representing two episodes in the eruptive history, both masses formed deep under ice of the continental glacier; in cooling there, the lava solidified in odd shapes.

Sunshine Coast

Probably a person has to live in Vancouver, with a climate that makes Seattle seem hot and arid, to consider this a "sunshine" coast. True enough, the rainshadow of the Vancouver Island Mountains shelters the Sechelt Peninsula, and the Coast Range is just far enough away that winds aren't yet being forced upward to cool and rain. Consequently, often one does indeed travel north in a rainfree corridor between two walls of black clouds, and sometimes the sun is shining. However, if we were serious about sun, we'd go inland to the Caribou Country. For us the joy of the Sunshine Coast is water—fresh water and salt water, in lakes and coves and bays and inlets, a maze of waterways occupying channels scooped out by Ice Age glaciers.

But take warning: though there is swimming on sandy beaches, and water-skiing and snorkeling, and digging for clams and picking for oysters and casting for fish, the road is always

either miles from the water, or houses line it wall to wall and accesses to the water are few. You're wasting your time to take this trip without frequently getting into a boat. Fortunately, many marinas rent them.

Views from highways are scarce, what with trees and houses in the way, and unless you rent a boat, the best views are from the ferries—the first one from Horseshoe Bay across the mouth of Howe Sound to Langdale on the Sechelt Peninsula, the second across Jervis Inlet. (If you want more ferrying, continue to Powell River and cross to Vancouver Island.) To visitors from Seattle the country seems newer and rawer than what they're used to. That's because it is. The Ice Age glaciers that melted away from Seattle 12,000 years ago hung around up there thousands of

Public dock at Sechelt

Indian pipe in Skookumchuck Provincial Park

reservations for motels, and to find room in a camp, it is best to arrive on Friday. Summer weekends here are all-around bummers. Half of Vancouver is up for the sun. No place to stay, long lines at ferries, no boats to rent, no way to get to the water except jumping off a ferry.

Trails are few and short. The one that fascinated us was the 2-mile path in Skookumchuck Narrows Provincial Park, leading to the outlet of Sechelt Inlet. With each change of tide the water pours in and out the narrow channel at the mouth of the 20-mile inlet, rushing like a mighty river in a giant rapids. To get there, drive to within ¾ mile of the ferry dock at Earls Cove and follow signs to Edgmont and the trailhead. Even if the rapids are absent, the trail through forest and past Brown Lake are reward enough. Logged half a century ago, the area now supports healthy second-growth rising tall above a carpet of moss and ferns. Note the moss-covered stumps notched for springboards on which lumberjacks stood, 5 or 10 or even 15 feet from the ground, swinging double-bitted axes and pulling the 8-foot saws unfondly called "misery whips." The day we hiked the trail in late July ghost-like Indian pipes were in bloom, a rare treat.

years longer. Wherever rock is exposed, their polishings and scratchings, roundings and pluckings and groovings are plain to see. One can look back in time to when ice as much as 10,000 feet thick buried these mountains, carved these bays.

Motels are clustered around the towns—from south to north, Gibsons, Sechelt, Pender Harbor, and Powell River. A few provide camping, as do three provincial parks. Every space is full on weekends; you then need

Tourist Information

Greater Vancouver Convention and Visitors Bureau, 650 Burrard Street, Vancouver, B.C. V6C 2L2, (604) 682-2222

Other Information

River rafting:

Whitewater Adventures, Ltd., 105 West 6th Ave., Vancouver, B.C. V5Y 1K3, (604) 879-6701

Reference Books

The Vancouver Guide Book, by Ginny & Beth Evans, Campbell's Publishing, Ltd., 201-1150 Rockland Ave., Victoria, B.C. V8V 3H7

Easy Hiking Around Vancouver, by Jean Cousins & Heather Robinson, publisher unknown

Lower Mainland Backroads, Vols. 1, 2, 3, & 4, by Richard & Rochelle Wright, Saltaire Publishing Co., P.O. Box 2003, Sidney, B.C. V8L 3S3

103 Hikes in Southwestern British Columbia, by David Macaree, The Mountaineers, 719 Pike St., Seattle, WA 98101

109 Walks in B.C.'s Lower Mainland, by David Macaree, The Mountaineers

Exploring by Bicycle: Southwest British Columbia & Northwest Washington, by Janet Wilson, Douglas & McIntyre, Ltd., 1875 Welch St., North Vancouver, B.C.

Exploring Garibaldi Park, Vols. 1 & 2, by Dan Bowers, Douglas & McIntyre, Ltd.

Exploring Golden Ears Park, by Dan Bowers, Douglas & McIntyre, Ltd.

Exploring Manning Park, by Robert Cyca & Andrew Harcombe, Douglas & McIntyre, Ltd.

Hiking Trails of the Sunshine Coast, Signpost Books, 8912 192nd S.W., Edmonds, WA 98020

Winery Tours, by Tom Stockley, The Writing Works, 417 E. Pine St., Seattle, WA 98122

Winery Tours:

Andrés Wines, 2120 Vitner St., Port Moody, B.C. V3H 1W8, Phone: (604) 937-3411, Hours: Noon-3 p.m. Tues.-Fri.; evenings 7 & 8 p.m., Tues., Wed. & Thurs.

Ste. Michelle Wines, Highway 10, 152nd St., Surrey, B.C. V3S 4N7, Phone: (604) 576-6741, Hours: Variable, but call ahead

Golf Courses in Vancouver

Burnaby Mountain Golf Course, public
Capilano Golf Course, private
Carnoustie Golf Course, public
Fraserview Golf Course, public
Gleneagles Golf Course, public
Greenacres Golf Course, public
Langara Golf Course, public
Marine Drive Golf Club, private
McCleery Golf Course, public
Meredian Golf Course, public
Musqueam Golf Course, public
Mylora Golf Course, public
Point Grey Golf & Country Club, private
Quilchena Golf & Country Club, private
Richmond Golf & Country Club, private
University Golf Course, public

OLYMPIC LOOP

Washington

Rolling Wheel Vacation

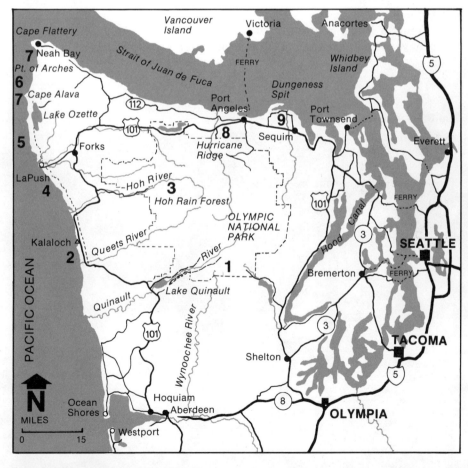

Third Beach, Olympic National Park

Ocean beaches to comb, rain forests to walk, wilderness to backpack, glaciers to climb. Elk, deer, mountain goats, and whales. A wildlife park, the nation's outstanding archeological dig, and a national historic site. And fishing, clamming, river-rafting, boating, golfing, and bicycling. What is this — the description of a continent? No, all these and more are condensed into the Olympic Peninsula. At the core is the enormous wildland of Olympic National Park, now more than "national" because the United Nations has designated it a World Heritage Park, a place of importance to all mankind, as well as other species that need a world to live on.

Many a Puget Sound resident has spent years of weekends and vacations exploring the peninsula without ever claiming to know more than a sampling of its wonders. All we can do is suggest an introductory tour that hits a few of the high spots.

Guided trips are popular on the peninsula, and various firms offer horseback riding, hiking, climbing, river-rafting, and fishing. Any guided activity that enters the national park must be licensed by the Park Service, which assures some degree of competence. For a list of current guides, write Olympic National Park, 600 East Park Avenue, Port Angeles, WA 98362.

Any season is great; summer is busier, of course, but winter isn't lonesome anymore because the ocean is then at its most exciting. The trip can be taken in either direction or in a

Blue Glacier on Mt. Olympus

Nature trail in the Hoh Rain Forest

series of zigzags and back-and-forths. We've described a 300-mile loop with many sidetrips starting from Interstate 5 and going clockwise from Olympia to Port Townsend.

Where to Stay

Motels of every size, shape, and price are located in cities, towns, and resort centers. Lodges at Quinault Lake, Kalaloch, and Lake Crescent offer an old-fashioned comfort and rusticity, a change in pace from motel life. There are campgrounds in state parks, Olympic National Forest, and Olympic National Park, plus commercial RV parks. At the height of the season many of the more popular motels and campgrounds are perpetually full, but somewhere in every area is sure to be a place to flop.

Forests

The climate makes the peninsula one of the greatest places in the world to grow big trees. So famous are the forests that those preserved in Olympic National Park draw visitors from around the world. It's not unusual, walking a crowded nature trail, to hear a number of languages.

So abundant are the trees outside the park, they support one of the most vigorous forest industries in the world. Between Port Angeles and Grays Harbor the highway is constantly a-thunder with the huge, swift logging trucks that so often terrify the tourist. Logs feed small cedar mills and large pulp mills—and are piled in wooden mountains waiting to be loaded on ships. From the highway one sees clearcuts in progress. By the Hoh River road a balloon lifts logs off a steep hillside. Forks, which claims to be the logging capital of the world, has an open-air exhibit of old logging equipment. On the Fourth of July the Aberdeen-Hoquiam community stages a logging festival with tree-topping, log-rolling, and log-chopping contests, a show not to be missed, especially since none of these ancient skills has any part in modern living.

Sad to say, the all-over-the-peninsula spectacle soon will taper off. Where sustained-yield harvesting is practiced, an even flow of forest products is provided indefinitely. However, vast areas of the peninsula are owned by private firms with no commitment to sustained yield. For years the forests have been overcut, and in the next decade the last of the old-growth outside the federal lands will be cut; until the second-growth is of harvestable size, much of the local population is going to have to move away. The peninsula faces decades of semi-ghosthood and

demands to harvest the national park.

Wildlife

Olympic National Park is thought to be home for the continent's largest population of cougar, plus great numbers of elk, deer, bear, coyote, whistling marmot, mountain goat, and a host of other beasts. Particularly unusual, unique in the conterminous 48 states, in the same park where goats are seen tromping across a glacier, seals are seen sunning on rocks just off the ocean beach, and gray whales migrating back and forth between Alaska and Baja California.

As for the birds, the Olympic coast may have one of the Lower 48's

Mountain goat beside the Blue Glacier on Mt. Olympus

Clam digging at Ocean Shores

largest concentrations of nesting bald eagles (see the "San Juans") plus a full array of sea birds and shore birds — in the same park as the full array of forest birds and river birds and mountain-meadow birds. The spring and fall migrations bring waterfowl by the skyful to Dungeness National Wildlife Refuge on the Strait of Juan de Fuca.

For a different sort of animal life, near Sequim is the Olympic Game Farm, where beasts are trained for Disney-type "wildlife" films.

Fishing and Clamming and Crabbing

The many rivers of the peninsula long have been famous for trout and steelhead. Lake Crescent, Quinault Lake, and Ozette Lake also are good sport; boat rentals are available at all.

Deep-sea fishing for salmon and a variety of other fish is done from charter boats operating out of Ocean Shores, Westport, Grays Harbor, LaPush, Neah Bay, Sekiu, and Port Angeles. For a list of charter services write the three chambers of commerce. At LaPush and Neah Bay you can rent a motorboat and venture into the sea on your own.

Surf-fishing has its fans—all that's needed, aside from the gear, is a stretch of beach. Any will do, the perch and whatnot are everywhere, as the ceaseless bird patrol testifies.

When the smelt are running, people dip them from rivers in buckets, washtubs, and hats, scoop them from the surf with nets. No skill is involved, one only has to find when the runs are in progress. Local folks always know. Crowds on a river bank are a clue. So are people in hip boots in the surf, wielding long poles with basket nets on the end, like butterfly nets.

Though several other excellent species of clams live in bays and on beaches, the razor clam sets the mob a-jumping. The subject of how-to is thoroughly discussed in "Oregon Coast" and "Long Beach"; as for where-to, the wide, sandy beaches north of Grays Harbor and around Kalaloch are mainly where the fans gather.

A sport for the expert is crabbing, pursued by the canny in the muds of Dungeness Bay at low tide. The non-expert ought to befriend a canny expert. Harvey Manning thinks one Dungeness crab is worth all the razor clams of Ocean Shores.

Beachcombing

The great big all-year Easter egg hunt at the ocean is the search for glass floats broken loose from fishing nets of Japanese, Russian, and other foreign fleets. When do the floats float in? Any time of year, unpredictably, but mainly in winter when big storms break up offshore congregations and carry them onto the beach. Our best luck was during a New Year's Day gale near Kalaloch, when we picked up 15 big ones in a few hours, all we could carry home. We saw other people with more—with cars and vans so full of glass there hardly was room for the greedy family.

Glass floats, prized though they are, are only part of the loot. The ubiquitous plastic floats make nice wall decorations, as do the gaudy ropes and nets of black and yellow and white and red polypropylene. Finally, it's always interesting to see what the freighter crews have been eating, as deduced from the garbage they toss overboard. On a single walk one may see garbage carrying printed words in several languages.

The best combing is not collecting but looking —in the tangle of kelp and seaweed left on the beach by the retreating tide and teeming with queer critters, and especially in tidal pools. To make your looking a thousand times more fun, do it in company of the books by Gloria Snively, Ruth Kirk, and Amos Wood.

At Kalaloch in summer a Park Service ranger-naturalist leads nature walks on the beach.

Are pretty pebbles your game? Neat shells? Driftwood? Plenty of them all.

Hiking

The hiking is superb in every season at sea level, and in every season there are short walks to enjoy and long backpacks. The car takes you to a hundred spots beside the ocean beach with miles of surf and sand in both directions. Other fine beaches line the Strait of Juan de Fuca, Admiralty Inlet, and Hood Canal.

The lowland rain forests also are magnificent in every season.

For the high country, summer and fall are best (unless you're an expeditioner equipped with snowshoes or skis and prepared to brave the wild whiteland). The trails of the National Forest and National Park climb to alpine meadows, moraines, and glaciers —and then quit so you can take off cross-country on your own.

A few walks and climbs and backpacks are mentioned in following pages. For in-depth discussions buy the guidebooks and the Olympic National Forest and National Park map (combined), 50c.

Bicycling

Due to the scary parade of logging trucks on Highway 101 and all too much by local residents, the loop is strictly for bikers with experience and icy nerves and fatalism. However, groups regularly do the loop, flags gallantly flying, begging for mercy. Actually the sidetrips are far more beautiful and relaxing—peaceful roads that lead to rivers, forests, and beaches. The way to make the best of everything is to drive the loop with bike on rack and periodically spend an afternoon or a day bicycling backroads.

Starfish and sea anemones in a tidal pool at Kalaloch

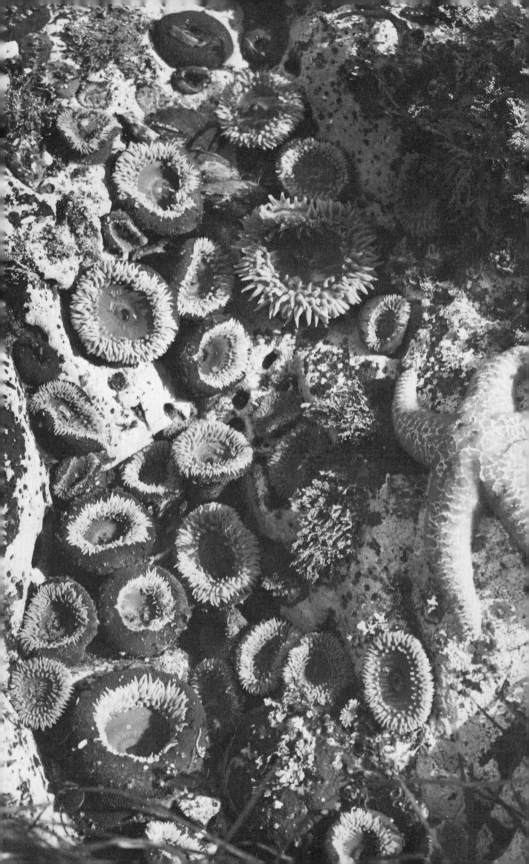

First Stop: Ocean Shores, Ocean City, Copalis Beach, Pacific Beach, Moclips

From Interstate 5 at Olympia drive 40 miles west on U.S. Highway 12 to the twin cities of Aberdeen and Hoquiam on Grays Harbor and another 20 miles on State Highway 109 to Ocean Shores, tourist center of the coast. Wide, sandy beaches extend north 15 miles from the entrance to Grays Harbor, perfect for clamming, surfing, golfing, fooling around in swimming pools, and generally doing the tourist trot. In fact, it is one of the two places in the state for which legal gambling has been proposed, the feeling being that if there's going to be a Reno in our sceno, why not here?

Another attraction, for those attracted here, is the plague of autos on the sand—which is why you don't want to bring your kiddies here to build sand castles.

The sand dunes, best in the state, are still another attraction for dune buggies.

To get away from it all, book space on a charter boat at Ocean Shores and go to sea and catch a salmon and lose your breakfast.

Frankly, if a nature-based vacation is your goal, get away from here fast. Or never go at all. Consider this a "sacrifice area," handed over to noise-makers in the hope they'll leave us alone elsewhere on the peninsula.

Quinault River road

Second Stop: Lake Quinault

Drive another 40 miles to Lake Quinault, from Ocean Shores on the beach road to Moclips, then inland to U.S. Highway 101. At the lake turn off on South Shore Drive. Stay at Lake Quinault Lodge (indoor swimming pool) or a campground (fresh air) and relax by the beautiful blue waters surrounded by green-forested ridges.

To fish or boat on the lake or river requires consultation with the Quinault Indians. However, it is possible to get on the water, probably —ask the Forest Service ranger.

The hiking is some of the best in the Olympics. An easy nature trail starts near the lodge at Falls Creek and goes through "Big Acre," a grove of monster trees many centuries old, and by rocks studded with a half-dozen species of ferns.

For a longer walk, drive the Quinault River road 15 miles upstream to the end and hike 3 miles through cathedral forest of fir and hemlock to the footbridge over the river, here flowing through a slot of fern-hung rocks.

For backpacking, the same trail goes another 10 miles to the Enchanted Valley Chalet, a three-story log "hotel" built in 1930 and surely the most impressive "log cabin" remaining in the Northwest. From the chalet the trail climbs to Lake LaCrosse, in meadows and snows and rocks 26 miles from the road.

River Floating

A float trip famous for years, ever since the Press Expedition of 1889, is down the Quinault River from Quinault Lake to the beach. Quinault Indians sometimes offer a ride that is exactly as good as in 1889, or thousands of years before, in a dugout cedar canoe. To find out if the ride is available during your visit, ask around locally.

In more recent years professional guides have come along with rafts. Regular trips are run down the Hoh River from rain forest to surf, and golly knows what else and where. Get a list of these guides from the Park Service.

Third Stop: Kalaloch

Drive 30 miles north to Kalaloch, beside the beach, with a lodge, cabins, and campground—all full in summer and most of winter. But a stop here is mandatory, maybe for hours, maybe for days. For some 10 miles the surf is never more than a few yards from U.S. Highway 101, though mostly screened by a dense thicket of trees and brush. However, seven trails lead to beaches that are connected at low tide, separated at high tide by rock points that set the waves exploding.

Gray whale from boat near Ocean Shores

The wide, sandy beach is good walking—and razor-clamming, and float-seeking, storm-watching. The tours from Kalaloch led by a ranger-naturalist are the best way to learn about the wonderful world of tidal pools.

The vista-point parking areas are dramatic in a full gale of winter, the surf churning and booming, literally shaking the ground and sending spindrift over the highway.

And then there are whales. In September and October see them headed south to breeding grounds off Baja, and in April and May going north to feed off Alaska. Watch for the spout and the occasional fluke or tail.

Fourth Stop: Hoh Rain Forest

From Kalaloch, U.S. Highway 101 goes inland. At about 25 miles turn east on the paved Hoh River Road 19 miles to the end at the Hoh River Rain Forest, with a campground and no other accommodations. But there is a fine little museum that introduces the rain forest.

The rain forest is most impressive and beautiful when seen in the rain—not too hard to arrange, since the annual precipitation averages 144 inches—*12 feet!*

Two self-guided nature walks lead through huge maple trees festooned with moss, giant firs, hemlocks, and spruces, and the carpet-like valley floor that is mowed regularly by browsing elk—which in winter are often seen near the museum.

The Hoh River trail leads 17 miles to the edge of the Blue Glacier on Mt. Olympus, highest peak of the Olympics. Achieving the summit requires a bit of experience and gear, or a professional guide.

Elk near Hoh River Ranger Station

Hoh River trail to Glacier Meadows

Fifth Stop: LaPush and Mora

Having returned from the Hoh 19 miles to U.S. Highway 101, proceed 10 miles north to Forks. A mile north turn west on the road to LaPush. In a little over 7 miles the road forks.

Turn left to LaPush

Three motels, one with a campground, and an RV park provide bases. The town itself, on the Quillayute Reservation, exhibits the relationship between Indians and newer Americans. Until recently, when federal conscience funds were appropriated, the original residents were consigned to poverty and lived in squalor, while the newcomers built a pretty Coast Guard Station, jetties to guard a fishing boat harbor, and profitable resorts. Slowly the Quillayutes are regaining their lands and water and fish.

Three rivers, the Soleduck, Calawah, and Bogachiel, join nearby to form the Quillayute River which enters the ocean at LaPush. The picturesque boat basin and the river-mouth jetty shelter charter boats and

Second Beach near LaPush

outboard-powered boats that go to sea, if that's what you have in mind. Indians sometimes will take you in dugout canoes through the surf and down the coast and back through the surf onto the beach.

At LaPush, paralleling the road, is First Beach, a nice walk. Before arriving at LaPush by highway, you'll pass parking areas with trailheads for Third Beach and Second Beach, both leading in a mile to strands of sand and vistas of cliffs and stacks and Asia.

The finest wilderness beach hike in the nation is from Third Beach south 16 miles to the end of the Lower Hoh River Road. See the guidebooks.

Turn Right to Mora

The Mora Campground of the National Park has abundant space in a lovely forest beside the Quillayute River and campfire programs on summer evenings. The road continues to a picnic ground at Rialto Beach, across the river mouth from LaPush.

One fine walk is south, along the jetty, ocean on one side, river on the other, to the channel between sea stacks and surf through which boats go to sea. Another is north a couple miles to Hole-in-the-Wall, a tunnel through a cliff.

The second-finest wilderness-beach hike in the nation is from Rialto Beach north 22 miles to Lake Ozette.

Sixth Stop: Neah Bay

Back on U.S. Highway 101, follow it toward Port Angeles 11 miles to the hamlet of Sappho and turn north on a road signed "Clallam Bay." Drive 36 more miles to the village of Neah Bay, on the Makah Reservation. In all your pokings about keep in mind this is private land. Visitors are welcome, but no hunting or fishing is allowed on the reservation, and nothing but photographs and memories can be taken from forest and seashore.

Motels and RV/tenter campgrounds in the town are popular with the fishermen who go to sea on charter boats or in small boats with outboard motors.

Cape Flattery makes a scenic afternoon. A private logging road, sometimes open to the public, loops around the headland. Remember that logging trucks have the right-of-way. A short trail leads to a viewpoint of the ocean and Tatoosh Island.

Shi Shi Beach and Point of Arches take a long day or short backpack. Drive the public road over the Waatch and Soos Rivers to where it dwindles to mudholes. Park before you get stuck and walk the final 2½ miles to Shi Shi, a wonderful half-moon of sand, and another mile to Point of Arches, a line of sea stacks jutting out to sea, perhaps the coast's best collection of tunnels, arches, and tidal pools. As with the English duchess who thought clothing was sheer mummery, and came to the ball wearing nothing at all, appearing delightfully summery, hikers to Shi Shi tend to go swimming without bothering about a bathing suit.

The unique feature of the Neah Bay area is the nation's most unusual **archaeological dig.** At Ozette, a site occupied by fishermen off and on for at least 2000 years, successive villages were engulfed in massive mudslides that buried and preserved houses and artifacts just as the ash of Vesuvius preserved Pompeii. Archaeologists presently are uncovering buildings and wooden tools, reed baskets and even woven nets, from 500 years ago, learning more about the evolution of the Makah culture than anyone ever thought would be possible.

First visit the museum at Neah Bay and travel backward in time, studying artifacts from the dig. The exhibits are so artfully done you feel you are actually there, in that ancient village.

To visit the dig, drive back from Neah Bay the way you came and take the sideroad to Lake Ozette. Walk one of the busiest trails in the state 3½ miles to the ocean and the site. The archaeologists have run out of money, and for now their diggings are closed. However, in a year or two the Makah Indians will open a small interpretive center at the site. For extended stays there is a National Park campground at Lake Ozette.

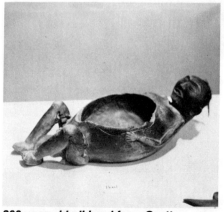

200-year-old oil bowl from Ozette

Seventh Stop: Lake Crescent, Port Angeles, Hurrican Ridge, Sequim, Dungeness Spit

After many a mile and, if the trip is done right, many a day, the route turns east from the ocean. There are still beaches, on the Strait of Juan de Fuca. But now there are mountain meadows, too. Return from Neah Bay to U.S. Highway 101 and drive east 50 miles, passing Lake Crescent, to Port Angeles, the first city since Aberdeen-Hoquiam, with every manner of accommodation and every amenity to coddle the tourist.

Is it a mountain lake? Is it a fjord? Lake Crescent has the feel of both, only a few hundred feet above sea level, high mountains all around, including 4534-foot Storm King, which keeps its snow most of the year. At the west end of the lake is a large Park Service campground and halfway along the shore is Lake Crescent Lodge, a restful spot.

Near the lodge is a small visitor center and the start of a 1½-mile nature trail through cool forest to 90-foot-high Marymere Falls.

Hurricane Ridge Visitor Center

Port Angeles

The city has the usual array of city delights. It also has the terminal for the ferry that crosses the Strait of Juan de Fuca to the English-like city of Victoria on Vancouver Island.

Ediz Hook is the spit that makes the port and city. Drive out to the gate of the Coast Guard station. Look north over the waters to Canada. Look south over the city to the mountains. Watch mills pulping logs into paper and ships loading logs for transport overseas.

Hurricane Ridge

Stand in a mountain meadow amid alpine flowers and gaze far down to forested valleys, out over a maze of peaks and glaciers, one of America's largest wildernesses. See deer in the meadows. With a bit of effort, see mountain goats.

Drive from Port Angeles, following signs to Hurricane Ridge, climbing to the ridge top at 5225 feet. The visitor center is surrounded by wildflowers in season; mid-July to mid-August usually is the climax.

For goats, ask a ranger at the visitor center about their guided walks on nearby Klahhane Ridge and Mt. Angeles. If no walk is scheduled, ask directions; in the course of a day you may see 60 or more goats. They seldom come in view of the road but never have been hunted and haven't the least fear of humans. Treat them with respect—though friendly, they are wild and have sharp horns.

Sequim—Dungeness Spit

West 17 miles from Port Angeles is the Sequim Prairie in the rainshadow of the Olympic Mountains, "sun country." Visit the **Manis Mastodon** dig where bones of this great big relative of the elephant were

found in a bog. The importance of this recent discovery is that a stone ax blade was found imbedded in a bone, establishing that man was here when the mastodon was, some 12,000 years ago, while chunks of unmelted continental glacier still were littering the landscape. Visit Olympic Game Farm to see where "wildlife" movies get their trained animals.

Above all follow signs from 101 west to Sequim to a Clallam County recreation area and campground at the boundary of the Dungeness National Wildlife Refuge. Follow the short trail down to the beach and walk either part or all of the 5 miles to the tip of Dungeness Spit, and perhaps sidetrip 2 miles to the tip of its offshoot, Graveyard Spit. On one side of the spit—longest natural sandspit in the nation—is the rocky beach of the Strait of Juan de Fuca, sometimes with an ocean-size surf. On the other side, beyond the heap of driftwood on the spit crest (evidence of ocean-size surf!), is the beach of Dungeness Bay. In the migration seasons thousands of waterfowl rest here. In other seasons there are few birds but almost always seals swimming close by the beach in strait or bay.

Eighth Stop: Port Townsend

From Port Angeles drive U.S. Highway 101 west 35 miles to Discovery Bay and turn north on State Highway 20 another 8 miles to Port Townsend. Stay in a motel or one of the nearby state park campgrounds.

Once upon a time Port Townsend was the official port of entry to the United States and a contender for eminence as the metropolis of the Inland Sea. Imposing buildings were erected to house magnates transacting business with the world. Then the railroads came to Tacoma, Seattle, and waypoints and there went the visions of sugarplums. The magnates' loss was our gain, because with no recurring tearing-down and replacing, as happens with thriving cities, the past survived until such time as it was treasured. In a way, history is now the main business of Port Townsend, which has a dozen or more buildings on the Na-

tional Register and in its condition of fond preservation and careful restoration has the look of a Puget Sound city of the 1890s.

For the **history-book** tour, park anywhere on Water Street and buy a city map at any of a score of shops. Walk along Water, noting dates on buildings. At Madison is the City Hall built in 1891, now the county history museum. It is said the jail in the basement once housed Jack London. One of the stores formerly was a tavern where seamen and loggers with three sheets to the wind were slipped a Mickey, dropped through a trapdoor, and awoke far out to sea on a sailing ship, shanghaied. Walk up Washington Avenue by Victorian mansions and the courthouse.

For more history, plus seascapes and sea birds, visit **Fort Worden State Park.** Either walk the beach from town or drive through town to the park and beach. As headquarters of the defense of Puget Sound, early in the century, the fort was the most elaborate military installation in the state, as well as one corner of the Death Triangle whose guns awaited any foreign navy that might try to steam in from the Pacific to bombard Seattle. Along one side of the parade ground is Officers Row, elegant old mansions in meticulous condition, leased as residences. Sites of gun batteries overlook the Strait of Juan de Fuca and the entrance to Admiralty Inlet. At the tip of the spit between is a picturesque lighthouse.

From Port Townsend the Olympic Loop is completed by driving to Hood Canal then by ferry and bridge to Winslow and Seattle.

Old German Consulate, Port Townsend

Tourist Information

Grays Harbor Chamber of Commerce, P.O. Box 450, Aberdeen, WA 98520, (206) 532-1924

Ocean Shores Chamber of Commerce, P.O. Box 382, Ocean Shores, WA 98569, (206) 289-2451

Port Angeles Chamber of Commerce, 1217 E. First St., Port Angeles, WA 98362, (206) 452-2362

Other Information

U.S. Forest Service and National Park Service information and maps:

Olympic National Park, 600 E. Park Ave., Port Angeles, WA 98362, (206) 452-4501

Forest Service/Park Service Information Desk, 915 2nd Ave., Seattle, WA 98104, (206) 442-0170

Map

Olympic National Forest and Park, 50c

River Rafting

Northern Wilderness, 4027 Latona Ave. N.E., Seattle, WA 98105, (206) 633-3946

Rivers Northwest, 141 Eagle Street, Winslow, WA, (206) 842-5144

Reference Books

102 Hikes, by Spring & Manning, The Mountaineers, 719 Pike St., Seattle, WA 98101

Trips and Trails 2, by E.M. Sterling, The Mountaineers

Wilderness Trails of Olympic National Park & Olympic National Forest, by Robert L. Wood, The Mountaineers

Footsore 3, by Harvey Manning, The Mountaineers

Exploring the Olympic Peninsula, by Ruth Kirk, University of Washington Press, 4045 Brooklyn N.E., Seattle, WA 98106

The Olympic Seashore, by Ruth Kirk, Olympic Natural History Association, Olympic National Park, 600 E. Park Ave., Port Angeles, WA 98362

Beachcombing the Pacific, by Amos L. Wood, Henry Regnery Co., 180 N. Michigan Ave., Chicago, IL 60601

Beachcombing for Japanese Glass Floats, by Amos L. Wood, Binford & Mort, 2536 S.E. 11th, Portland, OR 97202

Exploring the Seashore, by Gloria Snively, The Writing Works, 417 E. Pine St., Seattle, WA 98122

Golf Courses

Aberdeen, Grays Harbor Country Club (206) 533-3241, private
Ocean Shores, Ocean Shores Golf Club (206) 289-3357, public
Port Angeles, Peninsula Golf Club (206) 457-6501, private

SAN JUAN ISLANDS

Washington

Rolling Wheel Vacation

A mountain range that was ridden over by glaciers 2 miles thick, rounding peaks on one side and plucking them steep on the other, gouging deep channels that then were filled by the in-rushing sea, now is an archipelago of 172 islands, heaven for a water vacation by ferryboat or small boat. An infinity of bays and islets await exploration under benign blue skies of the Olympic rainshadow. There's also walking on trails through forests and sea meadows, and bicycling on quiet backroads, and history and wildlife.

That we devote so little space to so enormous a subject is due to the existence of an excellent guidebook, *The San Juan Islands Afoot and Afloat*, by Marge Mueller. Don't go without it.

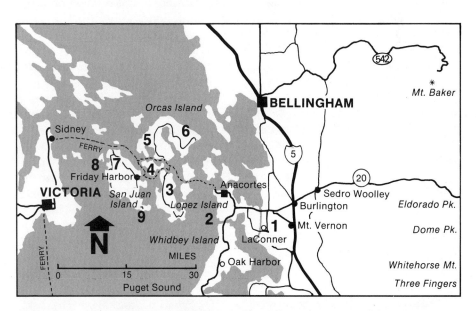

Ferry in Wasp Passage on the way between Orcas and San Juan Island

LaConner's waterfront, built on piling

Where to Stay

The vacation we describe begins with several tours on the mainland; the best plan, therefore, is to make first camp in Deception Pass State Park or an Anacortes motel, then catch the ferry next morning.

The first ferry island, Lopez, has only one or two small motels and only two small county park campgrounds. In the busy season you may have to sleep in your car and eat peanut butter sandwiches.

Shaw Island has no motels and a single county park campground.

Orcas Island is more like it. Rosario is luxury and history combined, a deluxe resort built around a famous old mansion, with tennis courts and Olympic-size pool, right next to trailheads and the fishing. There are other resorts and motels and cabin camps, mostly on the beach—in

season, reservations are essential. Moran State Park has several large campgrounds—in season, not large enough, so find a campsite in the morning if you want to stay the night. At Obstruction Point is a walk-in (½ mile) state Department of Natural Resources campground.

San Juan Island has a few motels at Friday Harbor and several resorts and motels scattered elsewhere. Roche Harbor is the feature, an impressive resort with rooms in the Hotel de Haro, built more than 50 years ago, and in cabins. The large swimming pool, tennis courts, marina, horse trails and horses to rent provide some visitors with all the vacation they need. The only camping on the island is at the little county park, which is always full.

Small-boaters have the best. Putt-putt or paddle to a non-ferry island with a state park, make yourself at home, and when the mood grabs you, putt or paddle to the next island home.

The "Mainland Islands"

People who don't know the area well tend to be very puristic about "San Juan Islands," confining that term to the islands in San Juan County, excluding everything in Island County and Skagit County. However, people who understand the geology and ecology and have a feeling for essence use a broader definition that includes Fidalgo Island, the northern part of Whidbey Island, and even extends inland to such "come-ashore" island as the peaklets around Sedro Woolley that now are surrounded by the Skagit Delta.

For us a San Juan vacation starts on dry mainland.

LaConner. Before the Skagit

Delta was diked and drained, the settlers had to stay on the high ground of "come-ashore" San Juan Islands. A group of these clustered beside the Swinomish Channel, the narrow waterway cutting off Fidalgo Island from the mainland, became the site of LaConner. Partly built on rock of the islets-peaklets and partly on pilings driven in the channel, some stores and houses date back to the 1880s. The Gaches Mansion, 1891, is open to the public on weekends. The Skagit County Historical Museum is chock-full of pioneer household furnishings, hand-wound gramophones, hand-cranked telephones, horse buggies, dolls, and more.

A walking tour through town entertains the visitor with history, artsy-craftsy shops (the town and vicinity shelter a sizable artists' colony), and boat-watching. Fishing boats still

Deception Pass bridge to Whidbey Island

unload catches, but most of the craft are pleasure boats racing to and from the "outer" San Juans. A "must" stop on the town tour is the Big Red Bridge to Fidalgo Island. Walk out to see Mt. Baker rising high and white above channel and town.

Deception Pass State Park. First an Army reservation, then a penal colony, finally given to the state and in the 1930s developed by the CCC under direction of the National Park Service, Deception Pass State Park wouldn't be at all out of its class as a *national* park. It has miles of beaches, including the largest sand dunes of the Inland Sea, and miles of trails, including one through the largest stand of old-growth forest beside a beach of the Inland Sea and another climbing to a summit with long views over seaways and mountains.

The park lies on both sides of Deception Pass, on Whidbey Island and Fidalgo Island. Connecting them, high above the channel that at turns of the tide is turbulent as a river, is a spectacular bridge that in itself is worth a visit.

Explorations are fully described in *Footsore 3*. A good scheme is to stop over in one of the campgrounds a night or two before catching the ferry.

The Four Ferry Islands

Washington State Ferries run daily trips from Anacortes through the San Juan Islands to Sidney, on Vancouver Island, with regular stops at Lopez, Shaw, Orcas, and San Juan Islands. The voyage is central to the fun of the islands. Have a map handy to identify each island, rock, bay, and channel you pass.

Some folks don't take a car on the ferry at all. They walk on, walk off. This limits on-island explorations.

However, other folks bicycle on, bicycle off. Island roads are never busy except near the ferry docks at ferry time, when cars whiz past as if on freeways. Most of the roads most of the time are peaceful, and all the islands are great biking—Lopez may have a slight edge. Rentals are available on Lopez, Orcas, and San Juan.

A ferry ticket gives stopover privileges, so all four islands can be visited on single round-trip ticket to Friday Harbor, on San Juan. At the dock be sure to get on the correct ferry, and in the correct lane, or else you won't be able to get off where you want.

One ferry a day goes on to Vancouver Island. It can only be boarded at Anacortes or Orcas Island. If you take a car, reservations must be made weeks ahead. For information, contact Washington State Ferries, Pier 52, Seattle Ferry Terminal, Seattle, WA 98101, (206) 464-6400.

Lopez Island. The first stop, Lopez, is sparsely settled, a few farms and one small village. It has no resorts, no exotic restaurants, no carnivals— and no crowds because few vacationers bother with it.

However, on dry land the bicycling is superb on miles of lonesome roads. On water the boater finds innumerable nooks and crannies of the shore that can't be gotten to afoot.

Shaw Island. Not an island for a vacation. Limited camping, few roads, fewer views, and no public access to the water.

Orcas Island. The island that has everything: campgrounds, trails, lakes for swimming and fishing, and a mountain whose summit you can walk to or drive to for one of the grandest marine vistas anywhere. The only thing it doesn't have much of is public access to the shore.

Resort-stayers and small-boaters have the beaches and bays to play on. For other vacationers the best of Orcas is on land, in Moran State Park, with two large fresh-water lakes plus several smaller ones, a waterfall, campgrounds, miles of hiking trails, and the lookout tower atop 2400-foot Mt. Constitution, so commanding and isolated a peak that on clear winter days it can be seen from hills near Seattle.

The center of park activities is Cascade Lake, warm enough in summer for non-shiver swimming. A twisty road climbs 6 miles to the top of Constitution. Steps lead to the top of the stone lookout tower and views over islands and waterways to five mountain ranges, north and east and south, including the range of which Constitution is a part. It used to be possible to stay on top as late as you liked, to see the lights of Bellingham twinkle in the night, but now a TV tower shares the summit and the gates are closed before dark. However, you can linger long enough to watch the sunset on Mt. Baker.

Perhaps the classic of the park's walking routes is the 3½-mile trail around Mountain Lake, from which a 2-mile trail leads to Twin Lakes, from which a 1½-mile trail climbs steeply to the top of Constitution. A neat way to do the trip is to hitch a ride up and walk back down, letting gravity do the work.

Deer are seen close up in the park, everywhere and constantly. They're not hunted and are no more afraid of people than of squirrels.

San Juan Island. Largest of the islands and most populous, San Juan is also fullest of fascinating his-tory. Here was "fought" the Pig War, last conflict between Great Britain and the United States, the two nations disputing which owned the island; the sole casualty was the pig. Here, too, may have been the last slavery in the United States—at least, some stories about olden times at Roche Harbor suggest that people were not free to leave jobs and homes unless the company let them. Another chapter in island history was the introduction of rabbits—actually, mostly Belgian hares and Flemish Giants—in the late 1800s by some thrifty farmer. As Australia has been cursed, so has San Juan Island—more of that in a follow-

Cascade Falls, Moran State Park

ing section. (But a blessing is the new private bus service on the island; in little vans labeled "Rabit Transit.")

Though Friday Harbor has begun to take on the look of a tourist trap, fishing boats still are based here; around the island they can be seen hauling in nets a stone's throw from the beach.

Close by are the University of Washington's Marine Sciences Laboratories. A person waiting for the ferry or staying at a Friday Harbor motel can walk the woodland trails and beach paths where professors and students relax from their studies.

San Juan National Historical Park is a national treasure on two counts: history and scenery.

The park is in two sections. At English Camp, where the "enemy" was based during the joint occupation —the years of truce that followed initial hostilities (killing of potatoes by the pig, killing of the pig by the potato owner)—are the original blockhouse and a poignant cemetery —none of the soldiers died in battle but some fell prey to disease and others drowned.

Across the island is American Camp, of which nothing is left but trenches theoretically dug to repel the English but actually just to look military; the two "armies" mingled on the friendliest terms. Here are the park headquarters and interpretive center. The walking is the most scenic in the archipelago, combining surf and driftwood with alpine-feeling meadows. Our recommendation is to take a whole day. Park at a lot soon after entering the park and walk the sandy beach. When beach ends in rocks jutting out in the waves, climb the ridge and return in the meadows, with views over waves and seaways. Watch out for rabbits—their tunnels are everywhere and you easily could break a leg.

Roche Harbor on San Juan Island

Echo Bay and Sucia Island

The Small-Boat Islands

Do the four islands by ferry and you've only got 168 others to go, by small boat. What kind of boat?

We're canoe people but must admit our craft isn't ideal for very much San Juan exploration. The kayak is better suited to the tidal currents that rush like rivers and the winds that come from nowhere and churn up rip-roaring turmoils. However, the consoling thing about canoe, kayak—or small boat powered by oars or outboard motor—is that if the weather grows fierce, you can pull up on dry land and wait for a calm.

Motorboating is pretty much a mystery to us, and frankly we don't care for the sort we see so much of in the San Juans; and we don't think the seals and otters and birds are crazy about it, either. To see the marine equivalent of a California freeway in rush hour, visit the San Juans on a holiday weekend.

Much to our surprise we learned that the many firms in Seattle and Anacortes that rent yachts with bunks and galleys will serve only *experienced* motorboaters. I guess all those crazy guys razzing around in big boats must own them.

The inexperienced can rent little boats, with little outboard motors, on Orcas and San Juan Islands, and that's the nice way to go. Take along camping gear, water, nautical charts, and maps that show the state parks. Slow down for paddlers. Watch out for idiots in monster machines and do a little island hopping, spending each night on a different one.

Bald Eagles

The San Juans abound with water birds. Many of the islets are in a national wildlife refuge to protect nesting grounds, and visiting these in nesting season is forbidden; be content with views from a distance. Even from ferryboats you'll see fantastic numbers of birds, especially if you have binoculars.

The raptors are the stars. More bald eagles nest in the San Juans than in any other of the original 48 states. We hardly ever visit without seeing one or more. Deception Pass has prime viewing—we once saw three mature eagles circling above us for hours.

However, San Juan Island is the hot spot. Driving across the island you'll see scores of rabbits; the bunny population surely must be in the hundreds of thousands. Birds with a taste for rabbit discovered this fact years ago and passed the word up and down North America. The number of bald eagles is incredible, and so's that of golden eagles and turkey vultures and hawks. On one drive across San Juan Island I spotted seven bald eagles, two on a snag close enough to photograph, two in the sky, the others on trees, blended into the branches.

June and July, when the young are being fed, have the best sighting. Binoculars are helpful but not essential. Most important is to know what to look for. Eagles are big birds that sit up straight when perched. Those with white heads and tails are mature bald eagles; those without the white are either immature bald eagles, less than four to six years old, or golden eagles. While driving those roads, I spend so much time looking at bumps on tall trees and snags, its amazing I've managed to stay out of the ditch.

Tourist Information

Anacortes Chamber of Commerce, 1319 Commercial Ave., Anacortes, WA 98221, (206) 293-3832

Orcas Island Chamber of Commerce, Eastsound, WA 98245, (206) 376-2273 or 376-4533

San Juan Island Chamber of Commerce, P.O. Box 98, Friday Harbor, WA 98250, (206) 378-4600

Reference Books

San Juan Almanac, Long House Printcrafters & Publishers, 2387 Mitchell Bay Rd., Friday Harbor, WA 98250

Exploring the Coast by Boat, by Frieda Van der Ree, The Writing Works, 417 E. Pine St., Seattle, WA 98122

The San Juan Islands, Afoot & Afloat, by Marge Mueller, The Mountaineers, 719 Pike St., Seattle, WA 98101

Footsore 3, by Harvey Manning, The Mountaineers

Golf Courses

Anacortes, Similk Beach Golf Club (206) 293-3444, public

Eastsound, Orcas Island, Orcas Island Golf Club (206) 276-4400, public

Friday Harbor, San Juan Island, San Juan Golf & Country Club (206) 278-2254, private

Bald eagle near the American Camp on San Juan Island

SEATTLE

Washington

Hub of the Wheel Vacation

If an indoor vacation is wanted, Seattle has the hotels and restaurants for it, and the theaters and museums and major-league sports. However, what sets this city off from others is the diversity of out-of-doors activities. Few indeed are the urban "hubs" where a person can spend a morning photographing wildflowers in a mountain meadow and that same evening watch sunset on waves of a saltwater beach, can leap a crevasse in a living glacier one day and the next day fish for salmon in the Pacific Ocean.

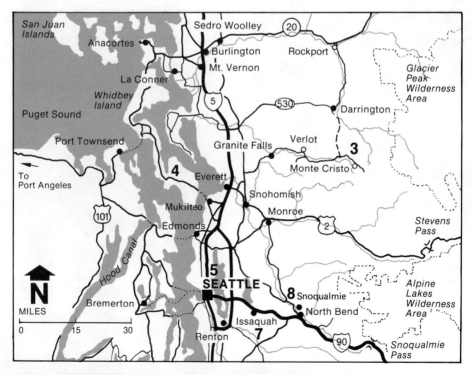

Mt. Rainier and Edith Creek near Paradise Inn

Where to Stay

Hotels and motels abound, and also privately-owned RV/tenter campgrounds; for information call Seattle-King County Convention and Visitors Bureau, (206) 447-7273.

Campgrounds of nearby state parks are small and usually full but within an hour's drive of downtown are many National Forest campgrounds; for location and space availability, call (206) 442-0170.

Sampling the City Out-of-Doors

Visitors from places less blessed often wonder that Seattleites ever go indoors at all (except to sleep or get out of the rain), there's so much to do in the outdoors. The guidebooks listed later cover the matter in detail. The following sampler suggests a very few of the great many experiences inviting the vacationer:

Alaskan Way. Walk the waterfront by shops and ships and fish and chips. Tour the Seattle Aquarium. Take a sidetrip to the Pike Place Market, one of the oldest surviving farmers' markets. Watch marine traffic and gulls from Waterfront Park and Myrtle Edwards Park.

Pioneer Square. Visit scenes of Seattle's turbulent past on the original "Skid Road." Take Bill Speidel's underground tour of Old Seattle— sidewalks and storefronts that are covered over and forgotten when the street level was raised.

Seattle Center. Lawns and fountains and shops. The Pacific Science Center. An elevator ride 600 feet to the top of the Space Needle and a

Seattle Center and Space Needle

Puget Sound and Olympic Mountains

panorama of city, Puget Sound, and mountains.

Woodland Park Zoo. The animal fair, all the birds and beasts are there, including those in a nursing home for injured eagles, hawks, and owls.

University of Washington Arboretum. One of the nation's largest and most important collections of trees and shrubs from the region, continent, and the world.

Burke-Gilman Trail. Walk or bicycle a popular trail along an abandoned railroad grade. Sidetrip to Gas Works Park on Lake Union, the University of Washington campus, the Marshland Trail on Lake Washington, and Logboom Park on Lake Washington.

Sampling the Waterways

Ferry to Bremerton. Take the ferryboat from the Seattle waterfront over Puget Sound to Bremerton, then the bus to the *U.S.S. Missouri,* the battleship on whose decks the Japanese armed forces surrendered in 1945.

Blake Island. Ride the little boat over the sound to a wilderness island. Walk the beach and forest trails, watch ceremonial dances in the authentic Indian longhouse, and feast on salmon baked over an open fire. The boat leaves from Pier 56. Make reservations by phoning (206) 329-5700.

Ferry to Victoria. Voyage to a city that seems to be a bit of England. Spend a full day or a whole vacation. The ferry leaves from Pier 69, British Columbia Ferry Company; phone (206) 682-6865 for sailing time.

San Juan Cruises. Several operators offer three-day boat tours to the San Juan Islands, spending nights at a deluxe resort. For brochures contact the Seattle-King County Convention and Visitors Bureau.

Exploration Cruises. Seattle is the home port of the Exploration Cruise Lines with two- to six-night cruises to the San Juan Islands, Victoria, and the narrow fjord of Princess Louisa Inlet in the wilderness of British Columbia. The cruise ships are specially designed to be beached, so passengers can go ashore for photography and exploration without a dock. For sailing dates and reservations ask your travel agent or call (206) 624-8551; from out of state, call toll free 1-800-426-0600.

Sampling the Country Around

Confused by the richness of choice? Perhaps a professional guide service is your answer. For information on firms active in white-water rafting, hiking, mountain climbing, horseback riding, and fishing, contact the Seattle-King County Convention and Visitors Bureau and/or the downtown office of Doug Fox Travel Service, phone: (206) 628-6161. Grayline Tours provides bus trips, with a guide's running commentary, through the city, around Puget Sound, and to Mt. Rainier.

Want to do it on your own? Maps and guidebooks treat everything from car-tripping and boating to hiking and climbing. Several gypsy tours may be suggested as introductions.

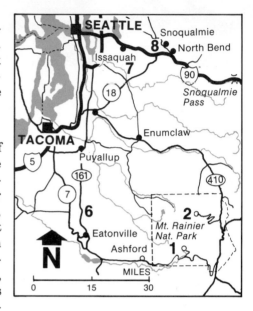

Mt. Rainier. The combination of maritime climate, elevation, and precisely the right latitude make the Cascade Range of Washington unique in the world for the juxtaposition of enormous glaciers and enormous fields of flowers. Other mountains have large glaciers but few flowers, or lots of

Mt. Rainier from a farm near Orting

flowers but little or no ice. Rainier must not be missed.

For a day trip, choose a day when the weather forecast is good; otherwise you may travel all around The Mountain and walk all over it and never see it. Drive to the Nisqually Entrance on the southwest corner of Mt. Rainier National Park and continue upward to the Paradise Visitor Center, elevation 5500 feet. Displays explain the park's geography and flora and fauna and how a glacier works. In season the adjacent slopes are a glory of color. Trails lead through flowers to views of glaciers. Then drive the Stevens Canyon Road past Reflection Lake, down into the Cowlitz valley, and climb back to meadows at Cayuse Pass. Sidetrip to Tipsoo Lake and views of Rainier. Follow State Highway 410 Seattleward to complete a round trip of some 200 miles.

In the proper weather that is a thrilling day. (Though perhaps exhausting —consider the bus tour as an alternative to driving a car.) However, at least several days are needed to get well into the mood of America's most massive chunk of real estate. There are four campgrounds in the park; space is hard to come by after noon, so stake out your spot early. National Forest campgrounds are located near the Nisqually Entrance and the north entrance. Outside the Nisqually Entrance is a small motel. In the park are Longmire Inn and Paradise Inn—a rustic old hotel of native woods built in the 1920s.

Top to bottom: *Avalanche lilies, Cascades golden-mantled ground squirrel, and ice climbing on the Cowlitz Glacier, Mt. Rainier*

A person planning to spend more than a day on the park's 300 miles of trails, should buy our guidebook, *50 Hikes in Mt. Rainier National Park*. For a starter try the Skyline Trail, climbing from near the Paradise Visitor Center 1½ miles through flowers to a 6900-foot vista point directly above the Nisqually Glacier—which is so active it currently is advancing. For a completely different perspective, drive to Reflection Lake and take the Pinnacle Saddle trail, climbing 1500 feet in 1½ miles to a dramatic view of Rainier. Steep snow may linger on trails well into August; before setting out, ask a ranger about conditions on the chosen route.

Wildflowers complete with glaciers for stares and gasps. As early as May the color bursts forth on ridges swept clear of snow by the winds, but winter stays in the meadows until mid-July and returns again in September, forcing the plants to compress their spring-summer-fall into two short months. The climax of the blossoming usually is early August —and a boggling sight it is. To identify

Climbing school camped below Mt. Formidable

the flowers, try our pocket guide, *Mountain Wildflowers.*

Mountain climbing, the ultimate in self-propelled sport, has no more popular goal in America than the top of Rainier. Climbers who come to The Mountain experienced in glacier travel and with the proper equipment and companions can choose from dozens of routes, easy to extreme. Climbers lacking the skills and/or companions can join a Rainier Mountaineering, Inc. guided party (two days) or attend the climbing school (five days, including the summit).

Hiking

What's your pleasure? Walks on beaches of the Inland Sea, or along lowland rivers, or on foothills of the Cascades with broad views of land and water? Look into the four volumes of *Footsore: Walks and Hikes Around Puget Sound.*

Or is it the Cascade Wilderness you seek, the giant forests and alpine meadows and sparkling lakes and summer snows? We have mentioned a few of our favorite short hikes, but if you want more we recommend (because we wrote them) the three books

Hikers near Cascade Pass, on a popular trail described in guidebooks

Fishing in the Skykomish River

that among them sample the whole of the Cascades: *50 Hikes in Mount Rainier National Park; 101 Hikes in the North Cascades;* and *102 Hikes in the Alpine Lakes, South Cascades, and Olympics.* For Mt. Rainier the 15 minute U.S.G.S. map is best. For Forest Service trails get a Mt. Baker-Snoqualmie National Forest map.

Monte Cristo. According to legend, the prospector who first gazed upon the outcrops of ore cried out, "Why, it's as rich as Monte Cristo!" That story turned out to have been invented, and the ore bodies found out to produce wealth only for stock promoters. However, the region surely is rich in craggy peaks, snowfields, rushing rivers, and virgin forests. No part of the Cascades is better for camping and hiking.

From Everett, drive east on U.S. Highway 2, turn north on State Highway 9, and then east through Granite Falls on the Mountain Loop Highway. At the Verlot Ranger Station, 12 miles from Granite Falls, stop for trail information and a National Forest map (50c). The valley narrows, peaks rise taller, and 33 miles from Granite Falls the pavement ends at Barlow Pass, elevation 2500 feet. Gravel road continues a final 4 miles to the site of Monte Cristo, 2700 feet, once the terminus of a railroad and the home of hundreds of miners, millworkers, and bartenders.

Campgrounds are numerous from Verlot to Monte Cristo, and so are trails. For any extended visit a person should have one or both of our guidebooks, *Trips and Trails 1* and *101 Hikes in the North Cascades.* However, no book is needed for an excellent introduction, the 1½-mile trail from Monte Cristo to Poodle Dog Pass and Silver Lake, set in a glacier-scooped bowl amid subalpine trees and fields of heather and huckleberry.

Whidbey Island and Fidalgo Island. A road map is sufficient guide to a superb day on and beside the salt water. Drive north from Seattle to Mukilteo and ferry to Whidbey Island. Follow the island highway to Ebey's Prairie, a National Historic Reserve on the oldest continuously-farmed land in the state, and beaches of Ebey's Landing and Fort Casey State Park, once part of the Death Triangle whose shore batteries guarded against enemy navies. At the north end of Whidbey Island explore beaches and forests of Deception Pass State Park. Then cross the bridge to Fidalgo Island and explore more of the park. By car take a sidetrip to the summit of Mt. Erie for long views out across waterways to the San Juan Islands, and another to Anacortes to see the ferries to the islands. Leave Fidalgo Island on the bridge over the Swinomish Channel to the Skagit Delta and visit La Conner to watch fishing boats unload. Stop by the Skagit Wildlife Recreation Area to view, in season, thousands of migratory water fowl.

Canoeing in Capitol Lake near Tumwater Falls

Kayaking on the Skykomish River

Bicycling

A number of shops (see the Yellow Pages) rent bicycles by the hour or day. The favorite ride in Seattle is the Burke-Gilman Trail, 12 miles on an abandoned railroad grade from Lake Union to near the north end of Lake Washington. A short connection on highway shoulders leads to Bothell and the start of the Sammamish River Trail, a magnificent dozen miles through riverside pastures to Marymoor Park on Lake Sammamish.

The serious cyclist must get the three volumes of *Bicycling Backroads*.

Canoeing

Canoes can be rented (see the Yellow Pages) by the hour or the day. Main waterways are too powerboat-crowded to be pleasant paddling. However, bays and nooks of the University of Washington Arboretum, on Lake Washington, are peaceful and quiet. If you avoid big-boat channels by staying close to shore, the north end of Lake Union offers enjoyable floating past small shipyards and funky houseboats. The open reaches of Lake Washington and Puget Sound are strictly for

the skilled paddler — and in settled weather — but are exciting challenges for experts.

Boating on Puget Sound

See the Yellow Pages. Every size of craft can be rented: cockleshells safe and fun for rowing in good weather near the shore; large outboard-motor boats suitable for crossing the Sound; and 35-foot cabin cruisers that can handle anything but the ocean when in the hands of experienced captain and crew (and these also can be rented).

The book for wandering Puget Sound and other arms of the Inland Sea is *Exploring the Coast by Boat*, describing state parks and privately-operated docks that offer overnight tie-up facilities.

The San Juan Islands are discussed elsewhere in these pages as a vacation in themselves. However, two tour boats from Seattle highlight the archipelago. One visits the outstanding resorts. The other emphasizes wildlife and carries a naturalist. For information contact Doug Fox Travel.

Under the Water

Puget Sound is among America's most rewarding areas for the scuba diver. For equipment rental and schools, see the Yellow Pages under "Skin Diving." Also see *141 Dives in the Protected Waters of Washington and British Columbia.*

White Water

No part of the nation has so many sporty rivers so near the homes of so many people. Kayaking and rafting are both so popular that boats are getting more common than fish. A visitor can get a good taste of the sport on a scheduled trip with a professional guide—contact Doug Fox Travel.

Fishing

Puget Sound, lakes, and rivers are all popular with fishermen, so popular that the fish regularly dumped in from hatcheries don't last long. Don't expect miracle catches. Still, an experienced fisherman can count on getting a few, and so can a lucky beginner. You will need a fishing license, sold at most sporting goods stores.

For the Sound, charter boats with skippers who know where to find fish are the best bet. Several companies schedule half-day or all-day trips. Check the Yellow Pages or the Seattle-King-County Convention and Visitors Bureau.

Wildlife

It is not uncommon in early morning or evening to see deer grazing beside a freeway. Coyotes live in Seattle parks and raid neighborhood garbage cans. However, more dependable wildlife viewing can be found at several spots.

The Seattle Aquarium on Pier 59 features a family of sea otters, as well as seal, octupus, and various fishes.

Chittenden (Ballard) Locks on the Lake Washington Ship Canal has a fish ladder with a viewing window. In season, big salmon swim right by the viewer's eyes on their way from the Pacific Ocean to spawning grounds on streams emptying into Lake Washington. In season, salmon fry or fingerlings swim by on their way out to the ocean.

The best place to see terrestrial wildlife is at Northwest Trek, specializing in animals native to the Northwest and providing habitats that are natural and unzoolike. Located near Eatonville on the highway to Mt. Rainier, the large, enclosed park has room for buffalo, elk, deer, bighorn sheep, moose, and mountain goat to roam free. There also is an exhibit of small animals. A visitor is just about certain to see river otter, beaver, raccoon, wolverine, skunk, and badger, each in its proper home.

For other wildlife, walk the Skid Road after midnight.

Beaver at Northwest Trek

Sky Sports

Hanker to ride as a passenger in a sailplane circling above peaks of the "Issaquah Alps"? Issaquah Skyport, east of Seattle on Interstate 90, just off Exit 17, will take you up.

Want to walk on air? At the same airfield is a parachute school that in a single day will teach you enough to do it safely, then take you up and drop you off.

Call Skyport airfield at Issaquah (206) 392-2121.

Steam Trains

Steam engine fans can take an hour-long ride, for a nominal fee, behind a 1926 Baldwin or spend their whole vacation "working" on a railroad at the Puget Sound Railroad Museum where volunteer help is needed to maintain 2½ miles of track and a 90-year old depot.

The railroad museum is in the city of Snoqualmie. The museum's address is P.O. Box 3801, Seattle, WA 98124, or phone: (206) 888-0373.

Tourist Information

Seattle-King County Convention & Visitors Bureau, 1815 7th Ave., Seattle, WA 98101, (206) 447-7273

Other Information

U.S. Forest Service and National Park Service information and maps:

Forest Service/Park Service Information Desk, 915 2nd Ave., Seattle, WA 98104, (206) 442-0170

Maps

U.S.G.S. Mt. Rainier
Mt. Baker-Snoqualmie National Forest, 50c
Ask for free list of all Forest Service maps.

State Parks information on camping, fishing and other recreational facilities:

State Parks & Recreation Commission, P.O. Box 1128, Olympia, WA 98501, (206) 753-2027

Mountaineering guides:

Rainier Mountaineering, Inc.
Summer address: Paradise, WA 98397, (206) 569-2227
Winter address: 201 St. Helens, Tacoma, WA 98402, (206) 627-1105

For other guide services contact:

Seattle-King County Convention & Visitors Bureau, 1815 7th Ave., Seattle, WA 98101, (206) 447-7273

Main Office, Doug Fox Travel, Inc., Vanderveer Building, 2819 1st Ave., Seattle, WA 98121, (206) 628-6161

Rental and sale of hiking, climbing equipment, and U.S.G.S. maps:

R.E.I. (Recreational Equipment, Inc.), P.O. Box C-88125, 1525 11th Ave., Seattle, WA 98188, (206) 323-8333

Reference Books

The Seattle Guidebook, by Satterfield & Dowd, The Writing Works, 417 E. Pine St., Seattle, WA 98122

Discover Seattle With Kids, by Rosanne Cohn, The Writing Works

Seattle's Super Shopper, by Priscilla Johnston & Dinah Stotler, The Writing Works

Winery Tours, by Tom Stockley, The Writing Works

Exploring the Coast by Boat, Frieda Van der Ree, The Writing Works

141 Dives, by Betty Pratt-Johnson, The Writing Works

101 Hikes, by Spring & Manning, The Mountaineers, 719 Pike St., Seattle, WA 98101

102 Hikes, by Spring & Manning, The Mountaineers

50 Hikes in Mt. Rainier, by Spring & Manning, The Mountaineers

Trips and Trails, Vols. 1 & 2, by E.M. Sterling, The Mountaineers

Footsore 1, 2, 3, & 4, a 4-vol. series of walks and hikes around Puget Sound, by Harvey Manning, The Mountaineers

Bicycling the Backroads, 3 vols., by Erin & Bill Woods, The Mountaineers

Mountain Wildflowers by Manning & Spring, The Mountaineers

Exploring Mt. Rainier, by Ruth Kirk, University of Washington Press, 4045 Brooklyn N.E., Seattle, WA 98106

Winery Tours

Associated Vinters, 4368 150th Ave. N.E., Redmond, WA 98052, (206) 883-1146
Hours: 9 a.m.-4 p.m. daily (call ahead)

Chateau Ste. Michelle, 14111 N.E. 145th St., Woodinville, WA 98072, (206) 485-9721
Hours: 10 a.m.-4:30 p.m. daily, except certain holidays

Manfred Vierthaler Winery, 17136 Highway 410 E., Sumner, WA 98390, (206) 863-1633
Hours: Noon-6 p.m. Tues.-Sun.

Puyallup Valley Winery, 121 23rd St. S.E., Puyallup, WA 98371, (206) 848-4573
Hours: 9 a.m.-6 p.m. Mon.-Sat.; noon-6 p.m. Sun.

Golf Courses in Seattle

Broodmoor Golf Club (206) 325-5600, private
Glen Acres Golf Club (206) 244-1720, private
Interbay Golf Park (206) 283-3170, public
Jackson Park Municipal Golf Club (206) 363-4747, public
Jefferson Park Municipal Golf Club (206) 762-9949, public
Rainier Golf and Country Club (206) 242-2222, private
Sand Point Country Club, Inc. (206) 525-5766, private
Seattle Golf Club (206) 363-5444, private
Tyee Valley Golf Club (206) 878-3540, public
West Seattle Golf Club (206) 932-9792, public

LONG BEACH

Washington

Hub of the Wheel Vacation

Draw a straight line 28 miles long, level it with a grader, cover it with sand, put an ocean on one side and a bay on the other, and you've got Long Beach Peninsula. Only a mile or two wide, it combines views out to China, surf for playing, clams to dig and fish to catch and wildlife to watch, and about as much history as is found anywhere in the Northwest. And in summer it has about as many people as are found anywhere.

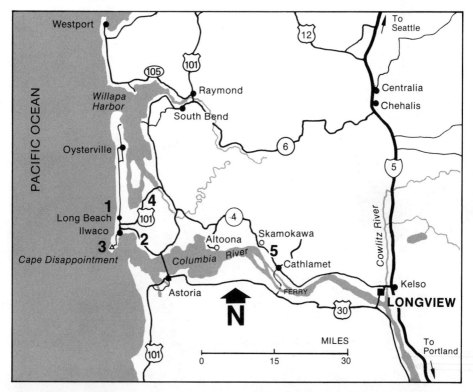

North Point Lighthouse

Where to Stay

The peninsula is a row of motels ranging from shacks to palaces, with rates to match. There also are numerous commercial campground and RV parks and several state parks—all usually full at peak vacation periods. Most accommodations are on the ocean.

A full array of restaurants, bars, amusement parks, and gimcrack shops compete for the vacation dollar.

History

Lewis and Clark slept here and so did a lot of other pioneers. Oysterville, founded in 1854, is named for its most illustrious citizen. Once the town had a population of 500, three hotels, a school, a church, and four general stores. Fewer than 100 people live here now, but some of the old buildings remain. The church was a gift to the community in 1892 by the city's co-founder (not the oyster). Near the church is a white-and-green house built in 1869, a yellow house from 1867, and a red house from 1871.

Though moved several times, the Oysterville Post Office has operated longer than any other in the state.

Ilwaco, Seaview, and Ocean Park have old buildings to show and old stories to tell.

Some of the best of the history is on the way to Long Beach. Going or coming, plan to drive State Highway 4 from Ilwaco to Longview and make two short detours into the Northwest past, visiting sleepy communities that were bustling cities early in the century. State Highway 403 leads to Altoona, where only a few pilings are left from the large canneries of old. This is the sort of place referred to as a wide spot in the road. But actually the road is squeezed very narrow as it passes through Skamokawa, whose chief edifice now is the schoolhouse. For a final interlude of olden times, at Cathlamet drive south on State Highway 409 and cross onto Puget Island, in the Columbia River, to see green pastures with picturesque farmhouses and barns.

Fort Canby and Fort Columbia are relics of old wars—or rather, old fears, because except for one Japanese submarine no enemy ever came within thousands of miles of their guns. Both are now Washington State Parks where visitors can muse upon the 19th century version of the MX.

Lewis and Clark camped just east of Fort Columbia, and the Fort Canby Interpretive Center has an excellent museum documenting their expedition from St. Louis to Pacific shores. There also is a small exhibit on shipwrecks and the history of the Coast Guard.

Oysterville church built in 1892

Beach Driving

People who go to the beach to walk the sands and listen to surf avoid Long Beach like a plague hole. In the 1930s, before attention shifted to salt flats in Utah, automobile speed records were set here. A walker, or swimmer, or sunbather sometimes feels they still are. After acres of clams were crushed and a tiny child building a sand castle, state authorities sought to ban machines from the beach. However, an outcry from local business people and a massive parking problem forced the ban to be partially lifted. Now a Washington State Supreme Court ruling that gives a constitutional right to run over clams, snowy plovers, and endanger children building sand castles has left even the partial ban in jeopardy.

Numerous spur roads give access to the beach. Just look for signs, "To Beach." Some lead only to beachside parking lots but others (if your car will float) go all the way to China.

Low tide obviously is best for beach driving, but remember that the tide comes in. Watch for soft sand that may catch your car and hold it for the ocean to finish off. After splashing, be sure to wash the salt off your car, top and bottom.

Remember that surf drowns out the sound of an approaching car—slow down for pedestrians. Be especially alert for children who have not yet learned to distrust adults. Do not drive in the sand dunes and stay away from Leadbetter Point—give the birds a chance.

Beachcombing

Long Beach gets as much in the way of driftwood, fishing nets, and glass floats as any other stretch of the ocean coast. However, there are a lot more people here to share the wealth than most places. Also, because of the beach driving, people are rolling up and down the sands all night looking for goodies.

Abandoned cannery on the Columbia River

So, this is not a decent place for beachcombing or beachwalking. You can ride a horse on the beach if you like but must bring your own—and it must be a steed trained to dodge speeding vehicles.

Bicycling

The roads are level—but mostly narrow and busy, leaving little good biking except on residential streets. The fact that no rentals are available on the peninsula says something.

Canoeing

Another statement about the place is made by the fact there are no canoe rentals. However, bring your own and actually escape tourists entirely.

Arms and inlets of Willapa Bay are excellent paddling at high tide. Repeat, "*high*" tide. When it goes out, it goes a long way, as much as a mile, perhaps leaving an unwary boater stranded on a mud flat for six hours. Viewing the enormous expanse of mud flats, one readily understands the need to watch the tides. But also to be watched are the tidal currents that rush in and out with plenty of power to upset a canoe.

Long Island, in the Willapa National Wildlife Refuge, has campsites only accessible by small boat or canoe. Rare, indeed, here are those who have driven reasonable people* off the peninsula.

*Harvey Manning

Clam digging on Long Beach

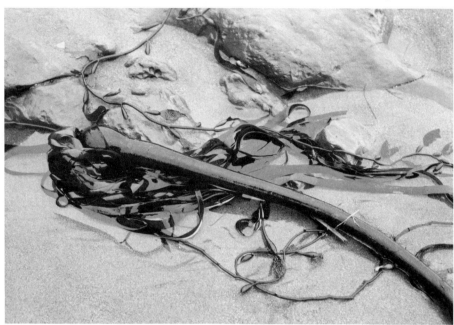

Kelp washed ashore by a storm

Clamming

Long Beach is the best place on the coast to pursue the razor clam, considered the most delicious of all seafoods by people who don't know any better. But give the mollusk its due— it's plentiful and easy prey for the unskilled who never would have a chance to catch a geoduck or a crab. Thousands upon thousands of meat-hungry clammers flock to the beach in season, wade in the cold water, dig holes in the cold sand, shiver in the cold rain and wind. If doing this in the company of thousands of people is your sport, this is the spot. (At this point we, the Springs, should point out that the above is the opinion of Harvey Manning. As for us Springs, we grew up on clams and love them, and someday will give the Mannings our mother's favorite chowder recipe and see if that doesn't change Harvey's mind.)

The Washington State Game Department sets firm rules on clamming, which you will learn when you obtain the required license from a local sporting goods shop. Also required are a tide chart (or simply follow the mob), a shovel (preferably the specialized species called a "clam gun"), a bucket, dirty clothes, and a lot of energy.

The clams live 2 to 3 feet deep in the sand near the low-tide mark. They are located by their breathing holes and are caught by digging faster than they can burrow deeper. Usually the hole fills with murky water, and you must reach down and grab the clam and wrestle it out. Wield the shovel too vigorously and you'll break the clam and mess it up for eating. (More clams are wasted than taken, and increasingly the Game Department is forced to close the season prematurely to preserve the species.) For more tips on technique see "Oregon Coast."

Canada geese on Willapa Bay

Wildlife

During spring and fall migrations the peninsula and bay abound with waterfowl stopping off on their way to and from the sunny south. Ducks, geese, and swans settle down by the thousands to rest and feed a week or two before resuming their journey. Quite a few geese winter in the area.

In summer there is much less to see. A few injured Canada geese usually are recuperating in a pond at headquarters of Willapa National Wildlife Refuge and are visible from U.S. Highway 101. The rare snow plover nests close to the shoreline at Leadbetter Point. The nesting grounds of this and other species at Leadbetter Point are off-limits to both motors and hikers, but the law is hard to enforce, and every year nests are run over.

While on the subject of wildlife, the Columbian White-Tailed Deer National Wildlife Refuge, located near Cathlamet, has several hundred of this subspecies that was common along the Columbia River when Lewis and Clark paddled by but now is endangered. The deer are not hunted and feed undisturbed while people watch from their cars. Best time to see them is morning and evening.

Fishing

Salmon. Ilwaco claims to be the salmon capital of the world, and from the looks of the harbor that may be true for the old 48 states. (A number of Alaska towns make the same claim.) There was a time when Ilwaco may well have been uncontested champion. In those days the Columbia River was lined with fish traps, and the canneries they fed still can be seen upriver from Ilwaco. Also in the old days there were no foreign fishing fleets sweeping the seas off the mouth of the Columbia, and no hydroelectric dams and reservoirs reducing the salmon runs to a pitiful remnant.

The modern, sporty way to catch salmon is to go on a charter boat operated by one of the dozen or more companies headquartered on the waterfront. Boats go out daily during the season. Reservations are advisable; and phone numbers of charter companies from the peninsula tourist office. You'll need a license (for sale in Ilwaco), warm clothing, either a lunch (calm weather) or seasick pills (normal weather), and a bit of luck.

Other Fish. Salmon may be king but other fish swim in the seas. No license is required for fishing in the surf or from the North Jetty. A heavy casting pole, bait, and hip boots or waders put you in business. For surf fishing, any spot on the beach is as good as another—as is evidenced by the winged fishers constantly patrolling the surf. Rocky headlands are extremely hazardous—if an extra-high wave (a "sleeper") doesn't get you, then maybe an incoming tide will, by cutting off your retreat. Jetty fishing also requires a watchful eye for sleepers but is secure from the tide. The North Jetty is easily accessible from Fort Canby State Park.

Lake Fishing. Peninsula lakes are well-stocked. You must bring your own boat, since none are rented locally, and buy state fishing license.

Surf fishing from Long Beach

Lighthouses

Two lighthouses on high bluffs at the south end of the peninsula guide ships into the mouth of the Columbia River.

North Point Lighthouse, built in 1899, overlooks Long Beach, its lens casting a beam of 1.2 million candlepower. Drive to Ilwaco, then go uphill, west, about 2 miles to a signed junction. Park in the small lot and walk the gated road ¼-mile to the lighthouse.

Cape Disappointment Lighthouse, built in 1856 to replace a system of white flags and bonfires, overlooks the Columbia. The top of the 53-foot tower is 220 feet above sea level. The original lens—a very complex glass assembly now at Fort Canby Interpretive Center—was 12 feet high and lighted by five wicks, 18 inches long, that burned five gallons of oil a night. From Ilwaco follow signs to the Coast Guard Station, park, and walk the steep ⅛-mile trail to the lighthouse.

Cape Disappointment Lighthouse overlooking mouth of Columbia River

Ilwaco boat harbor

Tourist Information

Long Beach Merchants Association, P.O. Box 503, Long Beach, WA 98631, (206) 642-2721

Reference Books

Exploring the Seashore, by Gloria Snively, The Writing Works, 417 E. Pine St., Seattle, WA 98122

Beachcombing the Pacific, by Amos L. Wood, Henry Regnery Co., 180 N. Michigan Ave., Chicago, IL 60601

Beachcombing for Japanese Glass Floats, by Amost L. Wood Binford & Mort, 2535 S.E. 11th, Portland, OR 97202

Wildlife Areas of Washington, by Schwartz & Spring, Superior Publishing Co., P.O. Box 1710, Seattle, WA 98111

Golf Courses

Peninsula Golf Club (206) 642-2828, public

SUN BASIN: VANTAGE TO MOSES LAKE TO LAKE COULEE

Washington

Hub of the Wheel Vacation

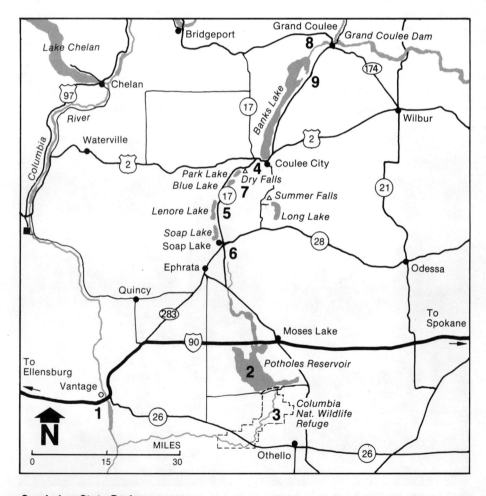

Sun Lakes State Park

Sun Basin

Here in the semi-desert kingdom of the sun are ample sagebrush and scabrock for hiking and horseback riding. There's plenty of lake water for boating, fishing, swimming, and wildlife-watching, too, because the "desert" is only "semi." However, the area is most notably distinguished by features found nowhere else. Some date from the distant geologic past (a rhinoceros cast in lava), others from the human past (an Indian sauna), and still others from the human present (one of the world's largest hunks of concrete). Dependably above in the big sky is the ever-loving sun.

Though more a "hub-of-the-wheel" than a "rolling wheel" vacation, several possible hubs lie along the way. The good things to do and see therefore will be treated with a bit of a roll.

Vantage

Accomodations are limited in the village of Vantage, where Interstate 90 crosses the Columbia River, but a pause must be made to gaze into the past.

Ginkgo State Park. When tropical forests grew in the Northwest, ginkgo trees toppled into marshes and were preserved first by water and then by flows of lava; over the eons the cellulose was replaced by silica, "petrifying" (agatizing) the logs. Chunks are displayed in the museum at Vantage. A signed path leads to the "petrified forest" where logs lie on the hillside. A map and permission from the park ranger are required to visit logs that actually stick up out of the ground, 2 miles away on the other side of the hill. Also of interest at the museum are pic-

Park ranger leading a group to a petrified tree in a remote corner of Ginkgo State Park

Air view of Potholes Reservoir

tographs that originally were on a cliff by the river but were broken off and brought here to save them from being flooded by Wanapum Dam.

Wanapum Dam. Downstream from Vantage the Wanapum Dam Tour Center gives fascinating insights into Indian life and tells the stories of fur-traders, soldiers, miners, and ranchers. A view window in the side of the fish ladder permits a close look at comings and goings of salmon, if any.

Moses Lake

Moses Lake, a small city on the lake of the same name, has Hallmark Inn with tennis courts, Lakeshore Resort Motel with boats to rent, other deluxe lakeside motels, and restaurants, theaters, and other urban amenities. On nearby Potholes Reservoir is a resort with housekeeping cabins and the campground of Potholes State Park. In the Columbia National Wildlife Refuge are several primitive camps.

As is true of all lakes in Sun Basin, fishing is good in early summer, then drops off as the water warms.

Potholes Reservoir. Before O'Sullivan Dam was built, the Potholes area was a wonderful vastness of sand dunes. The filling of the reservoir turned the dune tips into islands, great for camping. No drinkable water but a sandy beach is guaranteed. So is solitude because the islands are so numerous that every party can have its own. To get there, a little motorboat can be rented at the marina. The best craft in the shallow water is a canoe, but you have to bring your own.

Columbia National Wildlife Refuge. In spring and fall this refuge, one of the largest in the state, hosts thousands of migratory birds, including ducks, geese, and swans. There aren't so many in summer, but I've then seen mother ducks with a dozen ducklings apiece, terns diving for fish, muskrats swimming in ponds, hundreds of red-winged blackbirds, and clouds of gulls. Find the refuge entrance near O'Sullivan Dam.

Grand Coulee near Soap Lake

Sun Lakes State Park

The Grand Coulee

The centerpiece of Sun Basin is the 18-mile-long coulee sluiced out by catastrophic floods during the Ice Age, when an enormous glacier-dammed lake far to the northeast periodically broke the dam and roared through eastern Washington. The coulee remembers the flood times with a chain of seven lakes and many large ponds.

Traversed by State Highway 17, Grand Coulee has a number of spots to base a vacation. At Soap Lake and Blue Lake are motels, housekeeping cabins, and commercial campsites. Though not fancy, Sun Lakes Park Resort on Park Lake has an RV park and cabins and is ideal for fishing trip.

Finally there is the veritable oasis of Sun Lakes State Park, beside the sparkling waters of Park Lake, surrounded by lava cliffs. Canoes and rowboats can be rented, or you can

Sun Lakes State Park has guided horse rides and, on Park Lake, rental sailboats.

bring your own powerboat and water skis—or better, a sailboat. Riding stables offer guided rides of one to two hours. There is a nine-hole golf course with a scenic backdrop for every fairway—and miniature golf, too. Finally, the campground is the best there is for car explorations.

Dry Falls Interpretive Center. A visit here, where once the floodwaters thundered in a falls higher than Niagara and many times huger, is mandatory early in your stay. The displays explain the geological history, so a visitor then can understand what he sees elsewhere and tell the story of the Indians, some of whose past is still visible on the landscape.

For example; on walls of Grand Coulee are caves and overhangs the Indians used for shelter. Many can be seen from the highway; to explore

most, you must make your own way without help. However, a paved ¼-mile trail leads to the four Lenore Caves; find the short spur road to the trailhead between Lenore and Alkali Lakes. Note how the floors are covered with boulders that dropped from the ceiling—not, we hope, while the Indians were inside.

South of Soap Lake 3 miles is Coyote Sweat Rock, a large, hollow-centered granite boulder dumped by the glacier. Evidently the Indians built a fire in the hole and when the rock got hot, put out the fire, crawled in, and sweated. The mystery is what made

the hole. To get there, drive State Highway 17 south from Coulee City, cross State Highway 28, and in 2 miles reach a Burlington-Northern Railroad underpass. Park. Walk to the south side of the underpass and find a bulldozer track going eastward. Descend a short slope and find a faint jeep trail headed south almost parallel to the highway. Follow it ¼-mile to a pond and fence. The Sweat Rock is less than 100 feet farther.

The Lakes. Farthest down the coulee in the chain of seven lakes, Soap Lake is highly mineralized—though much less so than formerly. Indians

Cave shelter above Lake Lenore

and homesteaders and tourists have dunked themselves in hopes of relieving rheumatism, lumbago, arthritis, and other ills. Some people come because they just plain think it's fun to swim in the warm and buoyant water.

Before irrigation set lava-tube aquifers bubbling with Columbia River water, the coulee lakes were fed by seepage from meager rains and snows. The two lakes above Soap, Lenore and Alkali, were also mineralized in those days but now are almost normal.

The uppermost four lakes, Blue, Park, Deep, and Falls, are pure and clear and beloved by swimmers when the water warms up (the fishermen then give up).

Summer Falls. Where once glacier meltwater plunged, irrigation waters now tumble in Summer Falls. They do so in summer, that is, during the irrigating. From Coulee City turn south and follow signs.

The Blue Lake Rhino. More than 10,000,000 years ago a rhinoceros died in a lake that soon after was covered with molten lava that formed a cast, preserving the shape of the beast, though all that remains of its body is a few fossil bones. The rhino lay buried millions of years until Ice Age waters dug the Grand Coulee and its tributary, Jasper Coulee. Fortunate circumstance cut into the wall of the latter an opening just large enough to let a person peer in the cave that once was the space occupied by the dead rhino. Access is difficult—the site is on a narrow ledge on the precipitous wall of Jasper Canyon, most easily (not very) reached from Blue Lake by boat. Oddly, neither the National Park Service nor State Parks has shown interest in what probably is the only rhino cave in the world. (There also are unusual

Above: *Sunflowers in Grand Coulee*

Below: *Jasper Canyon and Blue Lake*

tree-cast caves.) Rangers at Sun Lakes State Park have been there and can give directions. Dry Falls Interpretive Center has a small model of the cave.

Grand Coulee Dam and Banks Lake (Reservoir)

Steamboat Rock State Park, on the shore of Banks Reservoir, is so new the trees give little shade, and the park rips off tent-campers by requiring them to pay for all the water, sewer, and electricity hookups installed for the RVers who truck along all the comforts of home. So, base this part of the tour southward at places already mentioned.

The Dam. Plan to spend at least a half-day. Start with the overall view from Crown Point Vista. To get there from the city of Grand Coulee, turn south on State Highway 174, signed "Bridgeport." In about 2 miles a sideroad leads to the high vista point on glacier-polished rock. After over-looking, return to Grand Coulee and drive to the base of the dam and the Visitors Arrival Center. Study exhibits showing how the dam was built and what it does, then take the self-guided tour past giant pumps, over the dam top above the 350-foot spillway, and down by elevator to the generators. To end the day, return in dusk to Crown Point Vista to watch an ever-changing light show on the dam.

The Reservoir (Banks Lake). The 28-mile-long reservoir is a central component of the Columbia Basin irrigation system, storing Columbia River water pumped by the dam up into what used to be a dry coulee. Steamboat Rock State Park, under steamboat-shaped cliffs that were an island during the Ice Age floods, is the recreation center. The day-use area is delightful. Facilities are provided for water sports. A 1-mile trail leads to the top of Steamboat Rock and magnificent views.

Grand Coulee Dam from Crown Point Vista

Banks Reservoir (Banks Lake)

Tourist Information

Soap Lake Chamber of Commerce, P.O. Box 433, Soap Lake, WA 98851, (509) 846-1821

Greater Moses Lake Chamber of Commerce, P.O. Box 1093, Moses Lake, WA 98837, (509) 765-7888

Reference Books

Wildlife Areas of Washington, by Schwartz & Spring, Superior Publishing Co., P.O. Box 1710, Seattle, WA 98111

Golf Courses

Moses Lake Golf & Country Club (509) 765-8131, private
Sun Lakes Park Resort (509) 632-5291, public

WALLA WALLA

Washington

Hub of the Wheel Vacation

Sun and water are the themes of vacations here. The Cascade Mountains, fending off wet clouds from the ocean, provide the sun. The Columbia River, draining glaciers and snowfields of a dozen mountain ranges, provides the water, which has been pooled up in reservoirs fit for boating, swimming, and fishing. If those diversions pall, there are a bicycle path along the Columbia, seven golf courses, the most interesting Christian mission in Northwest history, a desert with sand dunes, and a lonesome wilderness.

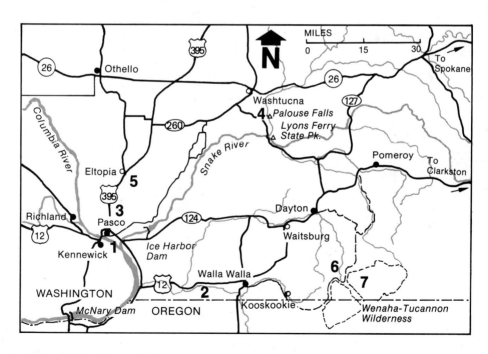

198-foot high Palouse Falls

Where to Stay

Hotels and motels are abundant in Walla Walla and, 46 miles away, in the Tri-Cities of Pasco, Kennewick, and Richland. In Richland, Holiday Inn has tennis courts, and International Dunes Rivershore is beside a golf course.

On Lake Sacajawea, the reservoir above Ice Harbor Dam, the Army Engineers provide several campgrounds of different sorts. Charbonneau is "developed," meaning it has showers and designated campsites and a ranger. We stayed a night at Windust, a "primitive" site where camping is allowed at one end of a picnic area. It's a delightful place, right by the shipping channel, and we watched barges pass as we cooked dinner. Unfortunately, "primitive" means un-

supervised, and a primitive teenage drinking party with screaming and primitive music kept the whole camp awake until 5 a.m. At "developed" camps one can sleep.

Near the Tri-Cities is a commercial campground. Fort Walla Walla Park has camping. So does Columbia Park between Kennewick and Richland, occupying 4½ miles of Columbia River banks, including the mouth of the Yakima River. It has picnicking, swimming, a children's playground, and a natural area with two interpretive trails designed by Lower Columbia Audubon Society. Our favorite campground is at Lyons Ferry State Park at the entrance of the Palouse Canyon, distant from cities but closer to the Blue Mountains and Hells Canyon.

Millpond at the Whitman Museum

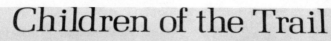

Children of the Trail

Travelers who n
usually drove o
farther west, af
food, medicine.

The Sager children
1844

ohn — Age 13 yrs.
cis — Age 12 yrs.
ine — Age 10 yrs.
eth — Age 7 yrs.
da — Age 5 yrs.
se — Age 3 yrs.
ta — Age 5 months

... But for seven children who arrived he
was a tearful homecoming. Their parents,
had died on the 2,000 mile (3,200 km) jou
six oldest children, shepherded by a ki
wagon train, pulled up here with the dil
wagon after seven arduous months on
Whitman greeted them with a smile, the
was "the prettiest woman we had even

The Sager baby arrived several days late
the Whitmans, who had lost their only
adopted all seven.

The 1847 Indian attack three years later made the Sager girls
orphans again. Among the killed were Marcus and Narcissa
Whitman and the two Sager boys, John and Francis. The victims
are buried together at the Great Grave.

Interpretive sign at the Whitman Mission

History

On October 16, 1805, 17 months after leaving Illinois, the Lewis and Clark Expedition arrived at the confluence of the Snake and Columbia Rivers, where now is Pasco. They camped two nights at the site of today's Sacajawea State Park. The Sacajawea Interpretive Center tells the story of the "Corps of Discovery" and its guide, a teenage Shoshoni girl. If it hadn't been for the horses supplied by her brother, a chief, Lewis and Clark might never have made it this far.

Fur traders were the next whites to reach this country. In 1818 they established the original Fort Walla Walla, or Fort Nez Perce, at the mouth of the Walla Walla River on the Columbia. A fort wasn't really needed then, but tensions grew as more whites arrived.

Historians love to argue about Marcus and Narcissa Whitman and their companions who in 1836 established the mission to the Cayuse Indians at Waiilatpu, a little way south of today's Walla Walla. For many years the myth was widely accepted that Marcus led the Great Migration of 1843 and saved the Northwest from the British Empire. The two Whitmans and the 16 others who died with them continue to be considered martyrs. The Whitman Mission National Historic Site, maintained by the National Park Service, has a museum where displays circumspectly discuss the total failure of the mission to save Cayuse souls, the personality conflicts the missionaries had among themselves and with the Cayuse, and events leading the Whitman Massacre in 1847.

A second and then a third Fort Walla Walla were built, the last in 1859, as bases for the Indian Wars —or as the Indians called them, the White Wars. Fort Walla Walla Park and the associated Fort Walla Walla Museum Complex recall that era. Operated by the Walla Walla Valley Pioneer and Historical Society, the complex preserves 14 pioneer buildings furnished with a collection of artifacts.

The city of Walla Walla, location of Whitman College, founded in 1859, was a sizable community when Puget Sound was nothing grander than scattered cabins and retains an air of graceful age. Three of its buildings are on the National Historic Register.

Before World War II the Tri-Cities were three farm hamlets. Whatever they may have contained of historical value was engulfed by the mushroom cloud of population growth that began with the plutonium works and never quit exploding. Very few visitors come from Nagasaki.

Boating

Any ordinary little outboard motor in a cockleshell is sufficient to voyage from TriCities up the Snake River on a stairway of reservoirs past Lewiston, until stopped by white water in Hells Canyon, or down the Columbia until stopped by surf breaking over Columbia Bar at Ilwaco. Each dam is detoured around via locks, no charge, courtesy of U.S. taxpayers. You'll share the locks with barges carrying grain down the river, oil up it. At night you can tie up at a marina or stop at any of the many Army Engineer and State Park campgrounds.

Sunshine Charters, Clover Island, Kennewick, WA 99336, (509) 582-3340, rents U-drive boats. If cockleshells aren't your style, they'll rent you a 40-foot houseboat.

If you have enough people to fill it up, or a fat enough bankroll to handle the charges by yourself, you can charter the 65-foot *Sun Princess*. (How much does it cost? As J.P. Morgan said when asked the expense of

owning a yacht, "If you have to ask, you can't afford it.")

Bicycling

Being a college town, Walla Walla has marked bicycle routes. Outside town are miles of quiet farm roads.

Pasco has a 15-block paved bicycle and walking path along banks of the Columbia River, starting at 39th Avenue.

Rentals are offered in Walla Walla by Sun Sports, (509) 529-9550, and Bicycle Bar, 529-7860.

Wine-Tasting

Many experts predict that the climate and soils of eastern Washington are such it eventually will surpass the wine regions of California and France. Since the advent of cheap irrigation water, Pasco has become a grape center, and miles of vineyards sprawl east of the city.

As noted earlier, a wine-tasting room is provided by Preston Wine Cellars, 5 miles north of Pasco on U.S. Highway 395.

Dams

McNary Dam on the Columbia River and Ice Harbor Dam on the Snake have visitor centers. See the boat locks in action. Look through windows to fish climbing ladders. Take self-guided tours of the powerhouses.

Hanford Science Center

In the Federal Building in the middle of Richland, "The Atomic City," the Department of Energy has exhibits discussing atomic energy, other sources of energy, and conservation.

Visitors are welcome at the Fast Flux Test Facility Visitor Center 11 miles north of Richland on Stevens Drive.

Palouse Falls State Park

Reason enough for a tour in this parched country is the 198-foot waterfall, a refreshing sight indeed. Several undeveloped trails can be explored. One circles the canyon rim to the top of the falls. Another descends a narrow slot in the cliff to the foot of the falls, an excellent place to see rattlesnakes.

The park itself is naught but a parking lot and a small picnic area. However, there is a campground at nearby Lyons Ferry State Park, where the Palouse River enters the Snake, now reservoirized by Lower Monumental Dam. Also here is the famous Marmes Shelter, a large cave used by prehistoric people and among the most significant archaeologic finds of recent years, radically reshaping ideas about the early years of man in North America. But there's nothing to see except an earth dam that was supposed to preserve the shelter from flooding by the reservoir. The Army Engineers built the dam as a political gesture, knowing all the while it wouldn't hold water.

Trail to the foot of Palouse Falls

Juniper Forest

Sand dunes up to 200 feet high, and sprinklings of juniper trees, extend over several square miles. Some dunes are anchored by plants, others are active, the sand beautifully rippled by wind.

From Pasco drive south on U.S. Highway 395, turn left and drive 24 miles on the Kahlotus Highway, signed "Kahlotus" and "Disposal Site"; if you pass a small yellow schoolhouse, you've gone too far. Turn left on a road confusingly named Snake River Junction; to the right it does go to the Snake, to the left is "Eltopia," or so the sign says. In 3½ miles turn left on Blackman Ridge Road, and in 2½ more miles left again on Rypzinski Road. Proceed past Loren Loeber Ranch (the friendly owner of the land you'll walk across, unless the privilege is abused and he is forced to put up "No Trespassing" signs) to road's end. Be sure all gates are closed behind you and watch out for rattlesnakes. There is no water and camping is not allowed. Motor vehicles are prohibited—though tracks show that a few sneak in.

The Juniper Forest is as controversial as it is unusual and beautiful. The Air Force once wanted to drop bombs on it, and motorcyclists and four-wheelers still want to roar around and rip up dunes and trees. Farmers want to graze cattle. Environmentalists want to preserve the fragile plant community just as it is and let it be enjoyed by people who value nature for itself.

Ecologically the forest is important, because though mountain juniper grows in alpine areas of Washington, and Rocky Mountain juniper in the San Juan Islands and elsewhere, the species here is western juniper, common throughout eastern Califor-

Juniper Forest. The "forest" is a scattering of western juniper trees.

nia and Oregon but at this point virtually at its northernmost limit. In addition 40 percent of Washington's ferruginous hawks nest here, as well as other more common hawks and owls. This is the only place in the state where scaled quail are found.

Blue Mountains

East of Walla Walla in the Blue Mountains is the Wenaha-Tucannon Wilderness, the lonesomest wildland in the state—except during the fall elk-hunting season. The Blues are rather dry, with small streams flowing through open forests that climb nearly to hilltops, but often not quite, leaving parkland meadows that in early summer are yellow with balsam root and glacier lilies and red with paintbrush.

In the forests calypso orchid blooms. Later, tiny cactuses blossom on foothills. In August the huckleberries ripen.

To explore, buy (50c) a map of Umatilla National Forest or the Wenaha-Tucannon Wilderness map at the U.S. Forest Service in Walla Walla. Ridge Drive, a forest road along the crest of a 6000-foot ridge with great views west to farms and east into wilderness, is reached from Walla Walla via Kooskooskie Road and then logging roads. The way follows the ridge 10 miles; drive as far as chuckholes and ruts permit.

The main appeal of hiking the Wenaha-Tucannon Wilderness is not lakes (there are none) or views (few) but solitude. Trails enter from all sides, but few people. For the best walking, drive from Delaney on U.S. Highway 12 to the end of Tucannon River Road. Try the trail up Meadow Creek and Panjab Creek to Indian Corral, 5½ miles, or the difficult Rattlesnake Ridge trail to the same destination. Other trails go to places with such interesting names as Grizzly Bear Ridge, Yearling Ridge, Crooked Creek, Smooth Ridge, Bear Wallow Springs, and Table Camp.

Hells Canyon

Hells Canyon can be floated down on raft or dory, as discussed in "Northeast Oregon." Quite a different experience is bouncing along the Snake River through the deepest canyon in the nation in a jet boat. Tours leave from Asotin and ascend the river 90-odd miles to the first impassable rapids. For brochures of the three or more companies running tours write the Clarkston Chamber of Commerce, Clarkston, WA 99403.

Blue Mountains

Tourist Information

Tri-Cities Visitor & Convention Bureau, P.O. Box 2322, Kennewick, WA 99302, (509) 586-4015

Walla Walla Area Chamber of Commerce, P.O. Box 644, Walla Walla, WA 99362, (509) 525-0850

Other Information

U.S. Forest Service map:

Umatilla National Forest, Pendleton, Oregon 97801

(also available at U.S. Forest Service station in Walla Walla)

Maps

Umatilla National Forest, 50c
Wenaha-Tucannon Wilderness, 50c

Hells Canyon boat trips. Boat operators and brochures available from:

Clarkston Chamber of Commerce, 749 6th Street, Clarkston, WA 99403, (509) 758-7712

Reference Books

Winery Tours, by Tom Stockley, The Writing Works, 417 E. Pine St., Seattle, WA 98122

Winery Tours

Hinzerling Vineyards, 1520 Sheridan Ave., Prosser, WA 99350, (509) 786-2163

Hours: By appointment only

Preston Wine Cellars, Star Route 1, Box 1234, Pasco, WA 99301, (509) 545-1990

Hours: 10 a.m.-6 p.m. Tues.-Sat.; 1-6 p.m. Sun.; tasting by appointment

Golf Courses

Kennewick
Columbia Park Golf Club (509) 586-4069, public

Pasco
Pasco Municipal Golf Club (509) 545-3440, public
Tri-City Country Club (509) 783-6014

Richland
Meadow Springs Golf Club (509) 783-1418, private
Sham-Na-Pum Golf Club (509) 946-1914, public

Walla Walla
Veterans Memorial Golf Club (509) 525-3483, public
Walla Walla Country Club (509) 525-1780, private

THE PANHANDLE
Idaho-Washington

Hub of the Wheel Vacation

What the Idaho Panhandle mainly has that vacationers flock to is lakes —three of the biggest in the Northwest, swum by some of the largest fresh-water fish on the planet. There also are mountains to hike and a mountain top to drive to, river rafting, bicycling, and an incomparable opportunity to study Indian culture. If interludes of city amenities are wanted in the course of an outdoor vacation, Spokane is close.

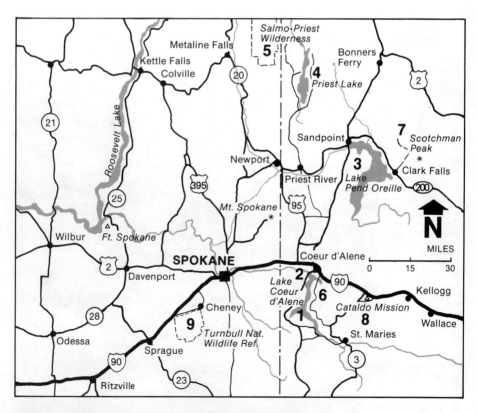

Pend Oreille River near the town of Tiger, Washington

Where to Stay

Metropolis or town or lake? Hotel or campground? Any number of hubs of many different kinds give easy access to the wheel and the many side trips that radiate from them.

Spokane has a profusion of hotels and motels and restaurants, fancy to plain.

Coeur d'Alene, a city on the north shore of the lake of the same name, has lakeside inns; around the 100 miles of shoreline are many resorts, commercial campgrounds, and Idaho State Parks.

Sandpoint, a city at the outlet of Lake Pend Oreille, features Edgewater Lodge, a lap of luxury on a sandy beach dandy for swimming. Around the 110-mile shoreline and on the Clark Fork River are resorts with cabins and RV parks, Farragut State Park, and National Forest and private campgrounds.

Priest Lake has such spiffy resorts as Hills Resort and Grandview Lodge with condo units and cottages, as well as three state parks and numerous National Forest campgrounds.

The gamut is from no-cost campgrounds to low-cost cabins to the plushness of Grandview, Rainbow Resort on Lake Pend Oreille, and Twin Lakes Village on Lower Twin Lake. For something completely different —a houseboat on Lake Coeur d'Alene —call North Shore Marine, (508) 664-9241, or Sun Up Bay Resort, 664-6810.

Edgewater Lodge and public boat ramp at Coeur d'Alene

The Big Lakes

The big lakes are Coeur d'Alene, 23 miles long, Pend Oreille, 43 miles, and Priest Lake, 25 miles.

It's boat country, obviously, and rental facilities will be discussed below. But note: If you bring your own boat from another state you must buy a special out-of-state license. If you have a Coast Guard sticker, buy a license at a marina; otherwise go to a county courthouse.

Lake Coeur d'Alene. By far the most popular lake—the most facilities and activities, the closest to Spokane, and therefore the most people. Boat-launch ramps, public swimming beaches, a carnival of fun and games.

The lake has many bays for exploring, and the Coeur d'Alene River is navigable for 24 miles. The St. Joe River and St. Maries River offer more miles of boating. A number of marinas rent motorboats, sailboats, and canoes by hour, day, or week; for a list write Coeur d'Alene Chamber of Commerce.

The *Mish-An-Nock*, a 300-passenger vessel, takes two-hour cruises on summer weekends.

Bicycling. A paved 7-mile bicycle trail goes from Coeur d'Alene to Hayden Lake; an extension to Lake Pend Oreille is planned. The trail runs along the east side of U.S. Highway 95. On the other side is a horse trail. Bicycles can be rented from Gordie's Bicycle Shop, 4055 North Government Way, Coeur d'Alene, (508) 664-9933.

St. Joe River entering Coeur d'Alene Lake

Hiking. A 1½-mile hiker-only trail climbs from Coeur d'Alene to Tubbs Hill, with broad views of the lake. The trailhead is in the free city parking lot by the water at the end of 3rd Street.

Lake Pend Oreille. Largest of the three lakes, 1100 feet deep, 43 miles long, and 6½ miles wide. Near the outlet is Sandpoint, a city of over 5000 people, well-situated for the fishing, hiking, and river-rafting discussed in following sections. In addition to the lake the Clark Fork River is navigable.

Most marinas rent powerboats by the hour, day, or week. You can

Flume used in 1930s and 1940s to transport logs to Priest Lake

cruise for a week, every night pulling into a different cove or marina. The Windbag, P.O. Box 1375, Sandpoint, (208) 263-7811, rents sailboats, wind surfers, and canoes. Several charter services offer lake trips with expert fishing guides.

Priest Lake. Most northerly of the three big ones, Priest Lake actually is two lakes, Upper Priest and Priest, connected by The Thorofare, a 2½-mile river, flowing slowly and deep enough for boats.

Until 30 years ago the only civilization on the forest-ringed lake was a small logging camp at the end of a rough and dusty road. Lumberjacks dumped logs in the lake and floated them down the Priest River during spring floods. When the drive was over, the town of Priest River threw a monumental bash that left hangovers from Spokane to Missoula. The annual drives ended in the late 1940s when a dam blocked the Pend Oreille River, route to the mill.

Now? A complete little city has grown up, complete with golf course. Paved highways run on both sides of the lake. Sophisticated resorts cater to the construction and cure of more genteel hangovers than ever a logger knew. There's even a convention center.

Long mountain lakes such as this create their own winds on warm summer afternoons. Though the boating is excellent, beware of little ripples that may grow to whitecaps. Some resorts rent motorboats. Canoeing is best on Upper Priest Lake.

Fishing

Panhandle fishing is the stuff legends are made of. Priest Lake yielded the American-record Mackinaw trout, 57½ pounds. Lake Pend

A bateau used on Priest River by lumberjacks in the 1940s. The river is now popular with rafters.

Oreille lists a 32-pound Dolly Varden caught in 1947 and a 37-pound Kamloops in 1949. To be sure, those were the days of few fishermen, and it may be that trout never again will be let alone to grow to lunker size. However, there's plenty of water, plenty of fish, and not all minnows—it tells you something when the minimum legal size for a keeper on certain of the rivers is 13 inches!

All three of the large lakes are good fishing—it's thought that Coeur d'Alene has more kokanee now than ever before. Don't ignore the smaller lakes or the rivers. Licenses are sold at resorts and sporting goods stores.

River Rafting

Rivers of the Panhandle are fine rafting. The upper Coeur d'Alene is good for beginners. Priest River takes a bit more skill. Stretches of the 120-mile St. Joe River are strictly for experts.

Obtain free brochures on float trips from Idaho Panhandle National Forests.

Trips of three to four hours through Spokane River Gorge are offered by Pacific Northwest River Expeditions, Route 1, Box 14, Spokane, WA 99204, (509) 838-8461.

Hiking

The Salmo-Priest Wilderness, along both sides of the Washington-Idaho line has a variety of trails, some on big-view ridges, others in deep forest of hemlock and huge cedars. A single trip can sample both. To get there, drive the Upper Priest Lake road on the Idaho side or from Metaline Falls to Sullivan Lake on the Washington side. The trails are shown on the Kaniksu National Forest map.

View from East Fork Peak trail

A hike we haven't tried that sounds intriguing is the 3-mile Mineral Ridge Trail overlooking Lake Coeur d'Alene, passing old mine diggings. Drive Interstate 90 along the lakeshore, then turn south on U.S. Highway 95 Alternate to the trailhead near Beauty Bay. This, and other trails, are shown on the Coeur d'Alene National Forest map.

Our favorite hike is near the Montana border and goes to the top of 5987-foot East Fork Peak in the Scotchman Peak area. For this hike use a Kaniksu National Forest map. From the town of Clark Fork on Idaho State Highway 200, drive north on Lightning Creek road which soon becomes Forest Service Road 419. In approximately 9 miles turn right on Forest Service Road 1084. At 1½ miles turn right again and go 1 more mile to the trailhead. (This road was not signed when we were there and was blocked by a slide, so we walked an extra ½ mile.) The trail gains some 3000 feet with many switchbacks, starting in forest and ending on the rocky ridge with views and more views.

Spokane

Commercial and trading and cultural center of the Inland Empire that sprawls from the Columbia Plateau through the Panhandle into Montana, Spokane provides a change of pace during an outdoor vacation. To get around the hotels and watering places buy *The Spokane Guidebook*, by Barry Anderson.

The proper start is Riverfront Park, site of the 1974 World's Fair. Most buildings have been removed, leaving spacious grounds extending to Spokane Falls, impressive in any season.

Downstream on the Spokane River 3 miles from the city center is Riverside State Park. Walled in by the Palisades (columnar basalt), one loses all sight and sound of civilization and feels miles away in wilderness—a crowded wilderness, to be sure, because the campground and picnic area are popular, and the Bowl and Pitcher, a volcanic formation, is picturesque.

The Museum of Native American Cultures has the most comprehensive collection on view anywhere of Indian arts and artifacts. From downtown follow Spokane Falls Boulevard east. Turn left on Division Street, right on Boone, and right again on Pearl to the museum, located on a bluff overlooking the Spokane River.

Though the Spokane Tour Train is a fake, it feels semi-real, and the hour-long ride through city streets is fun.

A bicycle path goes along the Spokane River; at least three shops rent bikes.

Mt. Spokane State Park

North from the city, 34 miles, reached by driving U.S. Highway 2, is 5881-foot Mt. Spokane with a campground and foot and horse trails. A paved road attains the summit and 360-degree views from Cascade Mountains west to Rocky Mountains east. Try the sunsets—inspiring. Then gaze south to city lights.

Fort Spokane

Built in 1880 on banks of the Spokane River, Fort Spokane probably was the last Army post established in the nation to protect the cowboys from the Indians. Maintained by the National Park Service as part of Coulee Dam National Recreation Area, four of the fort's 45 buildings survive. The brick guardhouse now is the museum.

Top to bottom: *Riverfront Park, site 1974 World's Fair; Fort Spokane; and Bowl and Pitcher, Riverside State Park*

Cataldo Mission built in 1853　　　　　*Trumpeter swans, Turnbull N.W.R.*

Trails lead to other building sites. Nearby are three Park Service campgrounds.

To get there from Spokane, drive east on U.S. Highway 2 to Davenport, then north on Washington State Highway 25. Water dammed by Grand Coulee Dam backs up to the fort, which thus is an access to 145-mile Roosevelt Lake (reservoir). The vacation can go that way, west to Grand Coulee, or north into Canada and the Arrow Lakes.

Silver Valley

The Panhandle is infested with history. The best is in the mining country.

Beside Interstate 90 some 30 miles east of Coeur d'Alene is the Cataldo Mission, established in 1842 on banks of the St. Joe River. The present mission, an imposing structure atop a small hill, was completed in 1853. Nails were so scarce that much of the building is held together by wooden pegs.

Eastward on I-90 is Kellogg. There and in neighboring Wallace and Mullan are the richest lead-silver mines in the nation. You can't miss

them. The bare hills are gouged and littered. Mountains of waste rock, tailings, and slag dot the valley floor. The river is poisoned.

Start by visiting the Kellogg Chamber of Commerce for suggested tours. Among them: Bunker Hill Smelter in Kellogg; mining museum in Wallace; a drive through narrow streets of Burke; and if roads are passable, explorations of abandoned towns with gray-weathered, tumbling-down (or tumbled down) buildings dating back a century or more.

Turnbull National Wildlife Refuge

A family of rare trumpeter swans lives on marshy ponds of the refuge, also home to a wide variety of other water and song birds. Most of the refuge is closed to the public and hunting never is allowed. Near headquarters is a pool where white-fronted geese, snow geese, and trumpeter swans hang out. A 5-mile self-guided nature tour samples the habitats and their denizens.

Get there from Spokane by driving west on I-90. Take the Cheney Exit and go south on Cheney-Plaza road.

Tourist Information

Coeur d'Alene Chamber of Commerce, Sherman Ave. & 2nd St. (P.O. Box 850), Coeur d'Alene, ID 83814, (208) 664-3194

Sandpoint Tourist Information Center, 210 1st Ave. (P.O. Box 928), Sandpoint, ID 83864, (208) 263-2161

Spokane Area Convention & Visitors Bureau, W. 609 Spokane Falls Blvd., Spokane, WA 99201, (209) 624-1341

Other Information

U.S. Forest Service maps and brochures:
Idaho Panhandle National Forests, 1201 Ironwood Drive, Coeur d'Alene, ID 83814

Maps
Kaniksu National Forest, 50c
Coeur d'Alene National Forest, 50c

Brochures
"St. Joe River Float Trips," free
"Floating Upper Coeur d'Alene River," free
"Priest River Float Trip," free

River Rafting
Pacific Northwest River Expeditions, Rt. 1, Box 14, Spokane, WA 99204, (509) 838-8461

Reference Books

The Spokane GuideBook, by Barry Anderson, Backwater Corp., 7438 S.E. 40th St., Mercer Island, WA 98040

Hiking the Inland Empire, Signpost Books, 8912 192nd S.W., Edmonds, WA 98020

"North Idaho Fun Guide," E. 2038 Avon Circle, Hayden Lake, Idaho 83835, (208) 772-3953, $1.00 (sometimes given free at chamber of commerce)

Golf Courses in the Spokane Area

Downriver Golf Club (509) 327-5269, public
Esmeralda Golf Club (509) 487-6291, public
Hangman Valley Golf Club (509) 448-1212, public
Indian Canyon Golf Club (509) 747-5353, public
Liberty Lake Golf Club (509) 255-6233, public
Manito Golf & Country Club (509) 624-4308, private
Pine Acres Par 3 Golf Club (509) 466-9984, public
Spokane Golf Club (509) 466-2121, private
Sun Dance Golf Club (509) 466-4040, public
Sunset Par 3 (509) 747-9663, public
Valley View Country Club (509) 928-3484, public
Wandermere Golf Club, Inc. (509) 466-8023, public

SUN VALLEY AND SAWTOOTH NATIONAL RECREATION AREA

Idaho

Hub of the Wheel Vacation

The names sum up the area pretty well—a valley of the sun and mountains like the teeth on a saw. Rivers and lakes for rafting and fishing and swimming. Roads for scenic drives and bicycling, and trails for hiking and horseriding, fill out the picture.

There's so much to do that the big problem is where to start. Our suggestion is Mountain Hosts, Inc., a unique travel agency specializing in outdoor sports. Call or write or visit: 411 Main Street, Ketchum, Idaho 83340, (208) 726-7471. If you want a Himalayan trek or a raft trip down the

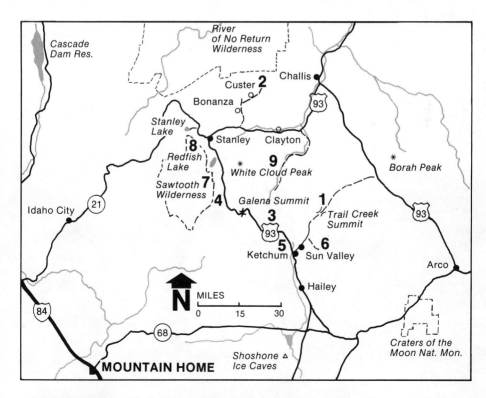

Redfish Lake, Sawtooth National Recreation Area

Sun Valley skating rink

Amazon, they can handle it. Primarily, though, they arrange reservations for local guide services and guest ranches that provide river rafting, horseback riding, air safaris, fishing, mountain climbing, backpacking, soaring, boating, tennis and swimming lessons—and if your vacation lasts into winter, cross-country skiing and dog-sled rides. The staff of Mountain Hosts is an encyclopedia of outdoor information and is as happy giving free advice to a lone hiker as planning a guided trip for a group.

Where to Stay

Fancy or plain, jet-setter or grubby old tent camper, there's a niche here for every vacationer.

Sun Valley and Ketchum and Elkhorn Village are the same place. The first is the resort, plush and expensive, offering golf, tennis, horses, bicycles, outdoor ice skating, and a large swimming pool. (The pool is reserved for guests, but everything else is open to the public.) The second and third are adjacent towns with motels and hotels priced high to moderate. Close by are two campgrounds, one commercial and the other National Forest. Both resort and towns have

Sun Valley Inn

Open air market held weekly at Ketchum

shops and art galleries and theaters. And restaurants, of course.

Stanley Basin, 60 miles away from the frolics in Sun Valley, is the center of mountain trails and lakes and rivers. Its dozen National Forest campgrounds have well over 1000 campsites—often all taken before noon. For indoor sleeping there are Redfish Lake Lodge, several motels, and such small guest ranches as the rustic Clark-Miller Ranch, which has a capacity of 30 guests, most of whom are repeaters from past years.

In the neighboring River of No Return Wilderness are wilderness ranches accessible only by raft, trail, and airplane. The heritage of old homesteads and mining claims, these private inholdings have accommodations from rustic to deluxe.

Reservations for the big resorts can be made through a travel agent or the local chamber of commerce. For the guest ranches and wilderness ranches it's best to deal with Mountain Hosts.

Scouting Around By Car

Getting behind the wheel and opening a road map are guaranteed to give a scenic day. Two tours are particularly recommended.

Trail Creek Summit. Before setting out on this auto adventure, check condition of the road (partly paved, partly gravel) with the U.S. Forest Service in Ketchum. Starting at Ketchum, drive the Trail Creek Road past Sun Valley, climbing 14 miles to 7894-foot Trail Creek Summit and a view to 12,655-foot Borah Peak, highest in Idaho. At 36 miles from Ketchum is U.S. Highway 93. Follow it south 40 miles to Arco and turn west on U.S. Highway 20/26 to Craters of the Moon National Monument, where the lava looks like it oozed out last week. Continue to the intersection with State Highway 75 and turn north to Sun Valley to complete the loop. However, if the day is hot, first turn south to Shoshone Ice Caves and Mammoth Cave, great places to cool

Redfish Lake and Sawtooth Mountains

Forest Service museum at Custer

off. Excluding sidetrips, the loop distance is about 200 miles.

Ketchum to Stanley. Don't miss this trip, 62 miles of paved road, not counting sidetrips. Follow State Highway 75 along the Big Wood River to 8752-foot Galena Summit and a glorious view of the Sawtooth Range, then drop to Stanley Basin. Short sideroads lead to Alturas Lake, Pettit Lake, and—the most spectacular—Redfish Lake. For one of the Sawtooth's most photogenic scenes, Stanley Lake, drive west from Stanley 5 miles on State Highway 21, then 3½ miles on Stanley Lake Creek Road (gravel).

Ghost Towns

From the 1860s to the 1940s this section of Idaho was prowled and dug and gouged and dredged by prospectors and miners, solitary and in mobs. They came and they went—and in leaving left behind ghost towns. All are on private property, and some are reviving as headquarters for a new generation of miners—and vacationers. Treat them all gently. Do not enter mine shafts—the timbers are rotten.

Custer. Thanks to the U.S. Forest Service, this is one of the best-kept ghost towns in the West. Little of the old town remains but what there is left now is being restored. A museum displays tools, household furnishings, and photographs dating from Custer's heyday.

Drive east from Stanley on State Highway 75 following the Salmon River to Sunbeam Dam. Turn north on Yankee Creek Road (gravel), passing miles of desolation where a gold dredge tore up the valley floor, and eventually pass the dredge itself, at the site of Bonanza. At 10 miles is Custer.

Sawtooth City. Nothing left but rotting logs and memories. The most interesting feature is how this once-thriving community has been reclaimed by nature. A bumpy, well-marked road near the head of Sawtooth Valley leads to the site.

Sawtooth Valley. Not only miners went away. To see ghost farmhouses, find a dirt road on the east side of Sawtooth Valley, starting about 1 mile south of the 4th of July Ranger Station and ending near Sawtooth City.

Boulder City. A well-preserved cluster of log cabins accessible by 6 miles of very rough jeep road that climbs 2500 feet. The way is best walked, and the meadows, small lakes, and views of Boulder Mountain make it a fine overnight hike. However, Mountain Hosts can arrange a jeep rental.

Abandoned farm buildings and Sawtooth Mountains

Drive north from Ketchum on State Highway 75 a little over 10 miles and turn right on Forest Service Road 158 (if you reach Easley Creek Camp you've gone too far). Follow 158, keeping right at an unmarked fork. Good road ends at a ford in ½ mile from the highway. Park here and follow jeep tracks 5½ miles to an intersection; go left to the ghost town, right to the meadows and views.

Bicycling

The Sun Valley bicycle shop, a few buildings east of the Sun Valley Post Office (don't confuse with the Ketchum Post Office), rents three-speed, 10-speed, and tandems, as well as bikes with baby seats. A paved trail connects Sun Valley and Ketchum, and except for main highways the streets and roads are quiet. The ambitious pedal all the way to Trail Creek Summit.

Hiking

The most popular part of the area is covered by *Trails of the Sawtooth and White Cloud Mountains*, by Margaret Fuller. You will also need a Sawtooth National Forest map. Several hikes there and in adjacent country are suggested as good introductions.

Sun Valley. Most of the many trails near the valley are buzzing with motorcycles and/or fly-buzzing horse droppings. However, two walks can be recommended.

Drive State Highway 75 north 3 miles from Ketchum to the Big Wood River National Recreation Trail. Watch carefully because the parking area is hidden from the road; the best landmark is a horse bridge over Big Wood River just up stream from the Hulen Meadows sign. The trail follows the river upstream a mile or more and

Bicycle path (top) *and horse trail* (bottom) *near Sun Valley resort*

then loops back, climbing some 1000 feet to a vista up and down the valley. Various loops can be made, yielding a walk of 2-4 miles.

Pioneer Cabin, built in 1939 for skiing, is on a high ridge with a commanding view of the Boulder Mountains. If planning to spend the night at the cabin, pack water and a stove. From the Ketchum stoplight drive Trail Creek Road 5 miles, passing Sun Valley resort, and turn up the Corral Creek Road 5 miles to its end and the trailhead. Climb the trail 4 miles, first in forest, then meadow.

Sawtooth Wilderness. The spectacular granite peaks and the sparkling lakes—plus the exclusion of motorcycles—have made this the most thronged hiking area in the Northwest. Trails to the lakes are crowded, particularly those from Stanley.

A good introduction is Bench Lake; from near Redfish Lake Lodge the trail climbs 1000 feet in 4½ miles. Our favorite hike is Sawtooth Lake, with a dramatic view of Mt. Regan. Drive State Highway 21 west from Stanley about 2 miles and turn left on Iron Creek Road to the trailhead. The way climbs several thousand feet in 5 miles.

Trail above Sawtooth Lake

White Cloud Peaks Roadless Area. Just east of the Sawtooths and included in the National Recreation Area, the White Cloud Peaks have mountains and lakes that many hikers consider even more beautiful than the Sawtooths. Unfortunately, the U.S. Forest Service has let the main trails become motorcycle raceways; most hikers prefer the mobs of the Sawtooths.

Nevertheless, Little Boulder Lakes cannot be ignored. Drive State Highway 75 east from Stanley past Clayton and turn onto East Fork Salmon River Road 16 miles to the trailhead. The Little Boulder Creek trail climbs 2 miles in sagebrush, then forest and meadows, reaching the lakes in 8 miles, gaining 2000 feet.

River Rafting

The Salmon River is one of the greatest rafting runs in the nation. It also is one of the most famous, so don't expect solitude.

For an easy sampler, several outfitters run two-hour and all-day float trips from Stanley. Reservations can be made the day ahead in Ketchum at Mountain Hosts or at Stanley.

For the wild river through the River of No Return Wilderness, runs of five to ten days are offered by 30-odd outfitters. Some groups camp out,

Castle Peak from Little Boulder Creek trail

others stay at wilderness lodges. A place in a guided party may be obtainable a day or two ahead, but it's safer to make reservations two to six months in advance, either directly with the outfitter or through Mountain Hosts.

Fishing

Some say the fishing is great; the man from California shown in the photograph returns every year to the same holes. Others say fishing is lousy —too many fishermen, all the holes are fished out by mid-July. Probably there always are fish for the expert and lucky. People who are neither might consider hiring a guide or going to a school; ask at Mountain Hosts. For nonresidents a one-day license is $3.50; one-week, $7.

Caught in Trail Creek, Sun Valley

Tourist Information

Ketchum-Sun Valley Chamber of Commerce, Box 465, Ketchum, ID 83340, (208) 423-5565

Other Information

Wilderness lodge and trip reservations:
Mountain Hosts, Inc., P.O. Box 2365, Sun Valley, ID 83353, (208) 726-7471

U.S. Forest Service maps and recreation information:
Sawtooth National Recreation Area Headquarters, Ketchum, ID 83340
Map
Sawtooth National Forest, 50c

Free booklet listing Idaho guides:
Idaho Outfitters & Guides Association, P.O. Box 95, Boise, ID 83701

Reference Books

Hiking Around Sun Valley, by Clarice Blechmann, Caxton Press, Caldwell, ID
Trails of the Sawtooth & White Cloud Mountains, by Margaret Fuller, Signpost Books, 8912 192nd S.W., Edmonds, WA 98020

Golf Courses

Ketchum
Bigwood Golf Club, 9 holes, public
Warm Springs Golf Club, 9 holes, public
Sun Valley
Elkhorn Golf Club, 18 holes, public
Sun Valley Golf Club, 18 holes, public

OREGON COAST

Oregon

Rolling Wheel Vacation

The most spectacular coast drive in the nation is Oregon's U.S. Highway 101. Ocean vistas come one after another without end, some from the edge of the beach, others from bluffs hundreds of feet above the surf. All beaches in the state are public, and so are innumerable viewpoints and beach accesses. There are wildlife and miles of flowers in mountain-like meadows, and fishing, clamming, beachcombing, hiking, bicycling, and river-running. The danger is trying to do too much in too little time. But no matter how busy you are, don't forget a kite—wind is good in every season, with never a powerline or tree to ruin the fun.

An entire vacation could be spent at any of the dozens of resort centers, cozy or Coney Island. Here we have focused on just four. As for which direction to travel, either will do fine, but the whole coast really should be driven both ways—seen from north and seen from south every landmark looks different.

Winter ought not be ignored. People are fewer than in summer and the weather is only a bit wetter and

Entrance to Depoe Bay

cooler; seldom is there snow, and seldom a day without at least some sun. The surf is far more dramatic—the most mind-boggling of ocean experiences is a winter storm.

Where to Stay

The choice includes fabulous inns famous around the world for luxury and prices, inexpensive motels, cabins with kitchens, state park campgrounds and commercial RV/tenter campgrounds.

Of the 18 state parks on the coast with campgrounds, reservations can be made at eight—Fort Stevens, Cape Lookout, Beverly Beach, South Beach, Beachside, J.M. Honeyman, Sunset Bay, and Harris Beach. For information and applications phone

Oregon State Parks Campsite Information Center, (503) 238-7488 (in Oregon, toll free, 1-800-452-5687) or write 525 Trade Street S.E., Salem, OR 97310. Reservations are recommended for July and August. However, though the parks fill early, if willing to make camp before 10 in the morning, you'll likely find a spot.

The advantage of motels over camping is a safe place to store belongings. Nowhere are cars burglarized more commonly than on the Oregon Coast. Locking the car, essential though it is to keep out amateurs, is no defense against professionals, who open doors as quickly with lockpicks as an honest person does with a key. Hiding money and credit cards and pre-

Depoe Bay and U.S. 101 highway bridge

Heceta Head Lighthouse

cious jewels is fruitless—the crooks know the hiding places by heart and can frisk them all in a minute. When parking your car, leave nothing in it you can't afford to lose.

Fishing

An Oregon angling license is required for any game fish. It may be obtained from sporting goods stores and Game Department offices.

Sea Fishing. Virtually every port harbors charter boats whose crews can teach the rankest of beginners to catch salmon, tuna, or cod. Depending on the port and how good the fishing is, there are half-day and all-day sailings—though usually the boat heads for port once everybody has the limit. Reservations are best made the day ahead. Look in the phone book for charter services, or ask the local tourist office or your motel manager —often he can make a reservation.

Surf Fishing. Perch are the usual catch, though larger fish also take the bait. Ask locals what gear is best. Any sandy beach will do.

Jetty Fishing. Fishing off rocks and jetties is often good. Jetties are safer. Though a person has to watch out for the exceptionally high wave called a "sleeper," being trapped by an incoming tide is not the threat it is on rocks, which also are slippery.

River Fishing. Casting from riverbanks can bring in salmon. Casting or trolling from a small boat is more popular. On some rivers rental boats and fishing guides are available.

Lake Fishing. Most lakes near the ocean are well-stocked; for most you must bring your own boat.

Clamming

Clamming is Harvey Manning's idea of cruel and unusual punishment, but lots of people consider it great sport. Rather little skill is required—mainly the ability to distinguish the breathing holes of clams from the holes of other under-sand breathers.

Several species can be dug year-round in bays along the coast. These cannot move and just lay there

Barnacles at low tide   **Kelp washed ashore by storm**

waiting to be caught at any reasonably low tide by anyone with an ordinary garden shovel.

The razor clam is trickier. Found only on sandy, surf-pounded beaches, it only can be reached at a minus tide. The season varies from year to year but normally is closed July 15 to August 31 during the spawning season, a period when minus tides are few anyway. The recommended tool is a long, narrow shovel — a "clam gun" — which can be rented at many places.

The trick of the razor is that it can move up or down, though not sideways. When spooked by the approach of a shovel, it starts digging down, often faster than the gunner can pursue. The technique is to select a likely razor clam hole, push the shovel blade straight down on the ocean side of the clam, wiggle the shovel a bit, slide your hand down behind the blade, and pull out the shovel. If the sand is soft, feel around for the clam and grab. If the sand is solid, dig a hole a couple feet deep and then reach in. Keep the clam alive in a bucket of salt water until ready to cook.

Beachcombing

The best time for beachcombing is winter, when strong winds blow in treasures and fewer people are around to compete. However, even in the middle of crowded summer every high tide deposits things on the beach to be looked at and pondered. Mostly it's garbage from passing ships, but often exotic garbage from foreign lands. An excellent book on the subject is *Beachcombing for Japanese Glass Floats,* by Amos L. Wood.

Agates, petrified wood, serpentine, and garnets are found on beaches. The best locations are shown in *Rocks, Fossils, Minerals,* a brochure-map published by the Oregon Department of Transportation, available at any tourist office.

Hiking

Eventually there will be an Oregon Coast Trail extending the whole distance, on the beach where possible, inland on the frequent rocky stretches. Some segments are already built; spectacular walks have already become extremely popular. For details see *Oregon Coast Trail Guide Book.*

Some state parks have excellent trails. Those of Fort Stevens, Ecola, Oswald West, and Humbug Mountain State Parks are particularly good. See following pages for descriptions.

Other trails are discussed in *Oregon Coast Range Wilderness Trails.*

All the state park trails and existing segments of the Coast Trail can be day-hiked. However, some have campsites accessible only on foot; backpacking to these, even if only a mile or so from the road, can bring the reward of quiet and solitude.

Bicycling

Oregon has the best bicycle trails in the West—which may not be saying an awful lot.

One of the state's designated and marked bikeway routes is the Oregon Coast, 350 miles long. Where the highway is wide enough, bike lanes are marked on the shoulder; on narrow sections the motorist is warned to watch for bikers. Tunnels have warning lights that flash when bicycles are inside.

Fort Stevens and Seaside have excellent bicycle paths. Seaside may be the only source of rentals on the coast, so it's best to take your own.

View south from Cape Perpetua

First Stop: Astoria, Fort Clatsop, Fort Stevens State Park, Seaside, Cannon Beach, Ecola State Park, Tillamook Head

Astoria

Located on the Columbia River almost in sight of the ocean, Astoria was named for John Jacob Astor, whose employees founded a trading post there in 1811, the first American settlement west of the Mississippi. For an overlook of city and river and a spiral mural depicting the history of the region, visit the Astor Column. The column is easy enough to find, standing 125 feet high and plainly seen from everywhere.

Next tour the port, where you can watch freight boats loading beside the docks. Just upstream from city center is the Columbia River Maritime Museum. Moored there is the lightship *Columbia*.

Fort Clatsop

Drive U.S. Highway 101 westward from Astoria across Young's Bay and follow signs to Fort Clatsop National Memorial. Take in the exhibit room and audio-visual program at the

Loading logs at Astoria

Visitor Center. Then walk the short way to the fort, the winter home of the Lewis and Clark Expedition in 1805-06. The fort was cramped and damp and rotted away long before settlers developed an interest in history. It was rebuilt in 1955, using Captain Clark's own sketch drawn on the elkhide cover of his field book.

Fort Stevens State Park

Built in the 1860s to guard the entrance to the Columbia River, the fort was modernized in World War I and again in World War II. During all those years people wondered what enemy was expected to send an armada up the river to attack Portland. Then, to universal amazement, soon after Pearl Harbor a Japanese submarine surfaced and lobbed several three-inch shells at Battery Russell, giving Fort Stevens the distinction of being the only military installation in 48 states to be attacked in World War II. (A Sunday school picnic was blown up in Oregon during the war, but that was by a balloon bomb.)

Fort Stevens has a huge campground, a lake for swimming, miles of sandy beach, and more miles of hiking and bicycling trails. It also has Battery Russell to clamber around; gaze out to sea and in mind's eye train the guns on phantom navies.

Explore the *Peter Iredale,* a four-masted, iron-bottom, British sailing ship that went aground in 1906 with no loss of life but total loss of ship. Each year a bit more of the wreck is battered away by waves or just rusts

Fort Clatsop

away. It has plenty of company. The area around the mouth of the Columbia has caught something like 100 ships over the years and is know as the "Graveyard of the Pacific."

For self-propelled fun, on foot or bicycle, the park has more than 20 miles of trail; ask for a map at the park entrance. One also can walk south towards Seaside on the Oregon Coast Trail.

Seaside

Here is the official end of the Lewis and Clark Trail, where the expedition reached the ocean and spent many a day boiling sea water to obtain the salt needed to preserve meat for the long journey home. Here, too, by the side of a famous beach, wide and sandy, is Oregon's first and still foremost beach resort. Within city limits an amazing variety of fun can be had: walking, bicycling, horseback riding, fishing, clamming, tennis, bowling, golf (two courses), and touring an aquarium and an art gallery. Other sports for which the city is famed are strolling the boardwalk—and sitting on a beach to watch the girls stroll by.

Fishing. Surf fishing is as good in front of Broadway as on any remote beach. Salmon and steelhead are caught in Necanicum River, virtually in the center of town. Sea fishing is best done by charter boat out of Warrenton and Astoria. Within a half-hour of the city are several rivers and a dozen or more well-stocked lakes including, in Fort Stevens, Creep and Crawl, Coffenbury, and Crabapple Lakes.

Bicycles and clam shovels can be rented at Seaside at the Bike Shop, 325 South Holladay.

Cannon Beach, Ecola State Park, Tillamook Head

Cannon Beach is a popular resort town, more purely oriented to beach activities than Seaside and, due to the cliffs and sea stacks, more photogenic.

Just north of town is Ecola State Park, with fine hiking trails, including the one to Tillamook Head. The Tillamook Head Lighthouse, strenuously built in 1879-81 on an island just a few feet from shore, is very difficult to reach in good weather and

Digging clams and skating at Seaside

absolutely impossible in bad. Abandoned in 1957 as too expensive to maintain, the lighthouse is deterioriating toward an eventual fall.

Oregon Coast Trail. At this writing the Coast Trail is continuous for 62 miles from South Jetty at Fort Stevens to Barview Park on Tillamook Bay. From Fort Stevens to Seaside the way is mostly on beach with one detour into Gearhart. Then it climbs over Tillamook Head and descends through Ecola State Park to Cannon Beach. The way is on beach for 7 miles to the ascent and descent of Cape Falcon. Next the trail climbs to the grandest

Cannon Beach

viewpoint on the whole coast, the top of 1700-foot Neahkahnie Mountain. (For insight into the period when white settlers were destroying the Indian community, read Don Berry's gripping historical novel, *Trask,* featuring an epic ascent of the Neahkahnie.) Dropping again, the way follows the beach to Nehalem Bay, where one must either arrange to be ferried over or walk the road an extra 3 miles around. On the south side of the bay the route resumes on beach to Barview Park and the (present) end.

The beach is best hiked at medium tide or lower and in some stretches can only be negotiated at low tide. However, tides never are insurmountable because detours via highway are always easy. Supplies can be purchased at several stores. Camp can be made at state parks, on remote beaches, or in motels.

Several segments make excellent day hikes, particularly Tillamook Head (see above) and Neahkahnie Mountain. The latter trail requires a sharp eye to spot. Driving south, U.S. Highway 101 climbs to a high viewpoint on the side of the mountain. Just before the first paved lookout point is a large gravel parking area; the trail starts directly across the road. The well-graded path switchbacks steeply up windswept meadows of the mountain, marvelously alpine-like, a glory of flowers in season; the white line of breakers shines in the sun far below, and Asia is across the waters.

For a dandy little sidetrip take the 3-mile trail to the top of 3283-foot Saddle Mountain. Just south of Seaside follow U.S. Highway 26 toward Portland to Saddle Mountain State Park and the trailhead near the small campground.

Cannon Beach from Ecola State Park

Newport and U.S. 101 highway bridge   **Yaquina Head Lighthouse**

Second Stop: Lincoln City to Newport

U.S. Highway 101 turns inland south of Tillamook for some 30 miles. However, 11 miles from Tillamook a county road signed "Pacific City, Cape Kiwanda" loops out to the coast and back to 101. The way passes Cape Kiwanda, base for a fleet of 200 fishing dories that are launched from the beach right through the pounding surf. It's an exciting spectacle. A dory's engine is started on the beach, the boat is shoved in the water, and when the waves are just right, the fishermen jump in and turn up the throttle and blast through the oncoming breakers.

The "miracle mile" that Lincoln City once boasted has stretched out to several beach-side miles of accommodations, restaurants, shops, and tourist whatnots. Included in the assemblage are several super-deluxe inns with plush niceties and grand views. Salishan Lodge, to the south of Gleneden Beach, has to be mentioned —and stayed at, if you can afford the rates, and if your idea of a vacation is an 18-hole golf course overlooking the beach, a large indoor swimming pool, two gyms, a hydrotherapy pool, sauna, billiard room, playground, hiking trails, and outdoor and indoor tennis courts.

South of Lincoln City 10 miles is Boiler Bay, a small cove in the rocks distinguished by its namesake, a boiler that is the final reminder of the steam schooner *J. Marhoffer,* which ran aground in 1910. The boiler is only visible at low tide. That's also the prime time to prowl the tidal pools and spy on starfish, seaweed, tiny crabs, and myriad other sea plants and sea critters.

South 2 more miles, Depoe Bay is a spectacular little fishing harbor. Boats enter through a narrow cleft bridged by U.S. Highway 101, a fine viewpoint for watching marine traffic. Charter boats for deep-sea fishing are based here. There's also good fishing from some of the docks.

In another 6 miles is Devils

Punchbowl. At high tide the water is a churning cauldron. At low tide the tidal pools, fully protected from souvenir hunters, offer one of the best opportunities on the coast to observe marine life.

Yaquina Head Lighthouse is worth a stop any time, but especially in summer when offshore rocks are blanketed with nesting birds. From the north city limits of Newport drive the lighthouse road through a giant gravel pit. Park near the lookout. Walk around the fence until Right Island comes in view, close enough to clearly see the birds but not so close you'll disturb them. Binoculars will let you enjoy a sight seldom available from shore. In late summer train your glasses out in Yaquina Bay to spot brown pelicans fishing. Awkward-looking at rest, they fly and glide with amazing grace.

Newport has three very special attractions: the Undersea Garden, a busy fishing industry on the north shore of Yaquina Bay, and the Marine Science Center on the south side.

The Undersea Garden is amid the fish-processing plants, docks, and restaurants. If all parking spaces near the garden are taken, continue to a huge parking lot with a public restroom. When fishing is good, the waterfront bustles. At least one factory has a window to permit tourists to watch the workers. Fresh fish are for sale and also crab right out of the water—and right out of the steaming pot, ready to eat. If you prefer to catch your own fish, cast a line from a dock, or the South Jetty, or the beach, or hire space on a charter boat and go to sea.

Cross Yaquina Bay on the giant bridge and follow signs to the Marine Science Center, a headquarters for research by the U.S. Environmental Protection Agency, National Marine Fisheries Service, NOAA, and Oregon State University. Most of the center is closed to the public but the famous museum is open daily from 10 a.m. to 4 p.m. in winter and 6 p.m. in summer. In one shallow tank children aged two to 100 can hold in their hands such cuddly creatures as starfish, sea urchins, and clams. In another you can pet an octopus and feel its suction cups —but carefully, because octopuses bite.

Brown pelican at fishing dock   *Marine Science Center*

Third Stop: Oregon Dunes National Recreation Area

Driving south on U.S. Highway 101, the first part of the third "stop" is the Cape Perpetua Visitor Center of Siuslaw National Forest, where audio-visual programs explain the forces of nature that shape the Oregon Coast. From the center a 22-mile auto tour winds through the Coast Range, passing 19 interpretive stops. Whether doing the whole tour or not, be sure to take in the summit of Cape Perpetua, at an elevation of 1200 feet with an outstanding dramatic view of the coast to the south.

South 2 more miles on 101 is Strawberry Hill turnout, a great spot to watch seals sunning on a rock that is close enough for people to have a good look yet far enough to let the seals sleep.

Heceta Head has the most-photographed lighthouse on the West Coast. The best views of it are from 101 near Sea Lion Caves.

Sea Lion Caves is perhaps the only place in the nation where sea lions come ashore so close to humans. The owners have been very sensitive to the needs of wildlife, preventing disturbance. There always are at least a few sea lions in the caves and on rocky ledges—at times they gather by the hundreds, an awesome sight. Of additional interest, the main cave is one of the largest sea grottos known, 125 feet high, some 2 acres in floor area.

Darlingtonia Botanical Wayside is named for *Darlingtonia californica,* the California pitcher plant, or cobra plant, a rather rare species that captures and digests bugs in leaves of most unusual appearance. Growing in boggy areas, the plant is nearly the size of a skunk cabbage.

Sea lions near Sea Lions Cave

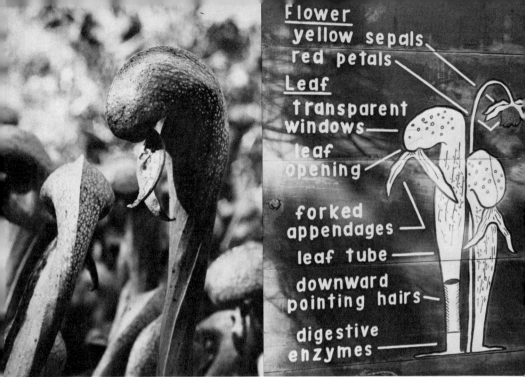

California pitcher plant (Darlingtonia californica) *and sign at the Darlingtonia Botanical Wayside*

Florence, at the mouth of the Siuslaw River, is proud of a fishing fleet, historic bay front, Pioneer Museum, and Doll Museum.

Here commences the empire of the sand, the Oregon Dunes National Recreation Area that extends 50 miles south, past the headquarters in Reedsport to the end at Coos Bay. Sand, sand, and more sand... Miles and miles of it piled in huge drifts—to be precise, 50 miles of sand, up to a mile wide, with dunes as high as 300 feet. They range from the classic Sahara-type, still on the march and showing the patterns of sand flowing in the wind, to inactive dunes anchored by grasses and flowers. There are dunes at the edge of the beach and dunes far inland, invading forests and killing trees. The varied scenery of the sand, the wildlife, and flowers make this one of the most spectacular sections of the Pacific Coast.

Jessie M. Honeyman Memorial State Park is the center of much tourist activity in the dunes. The park has two freshwater lakes, 240 tent sites, more than 100 trailer and RV sites, hot showers, and a sandy swimming beach. A ranger-naturalist puts on evening programs in summer.

Fishing

If the Chamber of Commerce is to be believed (and why should it lie?), the coast from Florence to Coos Bay has fantastic fishing in ocean, lakes, and rivers, and splendid clamming, too. Says the Chamber, the best things in life are free—free, that is, after you've bought a license, rented a boat, loaded up with bait, lost some hooks and maybe (at sea) your lunch.

Ocean fishing from beaches or jetties is for flounders, sole, and perch. Charter boats take you to sea for salmon. Trout and perhaps scrap fish are in lakes; some of which have rental boats. The Siuslaw, Umpqua, and Coos Rivers are for the elite of the Izaaks, as any stream fishermen will tell you.

Hiking

Oregon Coast Trail. The entire 50 miles are considered part of the Coast Trail and a grand part they are; because the highway skirts inland of the shifting sands and there are only occasional access roads and ORV playgrounds, most is essentially wilderness. The whole distance is frequently hiked — experienced beach pedestrians recommend doing it south to north to have the prevailing wind at the back, pushing. Camping is permitted on the beach ¼ mile or more away from paved roads or developed areas. For this, water must be carried; the alternative is to plan the trip to spend nights in state parks. The itinerary must take into account the need to cross Siltcoos, Tahkenitch, and Three Mile Creeks at low tide, when they can be waded, and at the Umpqua River either to arrange a boat crossing or detour inland through Reedsport.

Access trails to the beach from Crater Lake, Elk Creek, and Tahkenitch Campgrounds are nice

Beach strawberry in sand dunes

walks in themselves. The Tahkenitch trail starts in a fir forest with head-high salal and thimbleberry bushes crowned by 10-foot-tall rhododendrons. The way is well-defined in forest but obscure in the sand, so keep looking over your shoulder to be able to find your way back. A very primitive, little-used trail starts at Tahkenitch Dam. Find the unmarked trailhead on the north side of Tahkenitch Creek bridge. Either follow the creek around a big meander bend or go straight west to the river mouth — in that case pay attention to the return. Osprey and eagles frequently are seen here, as well as the rare snowy plover.

The **River of No Return Nature Trail** from Siltcoos Creek Campground follows an abandoned stream bed (thus the name).

The **Drift Creek Trail** leads inland to a remote camp near a good fishing hole. Ask for directions at Waldport Ranger Station.

ORV

This isn't our sport, so don't expect raves from us. Off-road vehicles destroy fragile plant communities, the exquisite shape of wind-sculptured dunes, and the peace and quiet of other-worldly sand lands.

While we have very little patience with the government for allowing public use of ORVs to crisscross their land (our land), we (Springs) must tolerate, and even recommend, ORV tours of the sand dunes by responsible commercial companies in their 12-passenger all-terrain vehicles. You will find one or more operators between Florence and Reedsport. Just don't let the drivers brainwash you into believing that is the only or best way to see the sand dunes. (And watch out for landmines planted by Harvey, who takes a purer view.)

Sand dunes at Jessie M. Honeyman Memorial State Park

Fourth Stop: The Southern Beaches

The coast from Bandon to Brookings has views to needle-like islands from the beach near Bandon, views halfway to the edge of the world from heights near Humbug Mountain, hiking, beachcombing, and some of the finest white-water river runs in the West. Base for explorations can be made at motels in any of the towns or campgrounds scattered along the way.

Hiking

Being built half-mile by half-mile with volunteer labor, the Oregon Coast Trail is coming along slowly, but coming—ask locally for late reports on progress.

Some of the beach south of Bandon is walkable and, with the road several miles inland, gives a sense of remoteness only occasionally interrupted by farms or houses. Try a bivouac hike: spend two to three days walking with a day pack, going inland to 101 in the afternoon to bivouac at the first handy motel; at trip's end catch a bus back to your car; but maybe scout the bivouacs first by car and make reservations.

A 3-mile trail climbs 1750-foot Humbug Mountain.

The **Kalmiopsis Wilderness,** famed for botanical rarities, has good trails—a bit hot in summer, maybe. The best is the Boulder Creek trail that crosses the wilderness, several times descending to the Chetco River, whose water is unbelievably clear.

Fishing

For deep-sea fishing take a charter boat at Gold Beach. The harbor jetty has good spots to cast a line. At Bandon fish a freshwater lake—and/or rent a crab pot. There are rivers, too.

Bandon Needles

White Water

Gold Beach is the end of the line for the rafting trips down the Rogue River that start near Grants Pass (see "Rogue River") and jumping-off place for powerboat trips up the Rogue. At least three companies offer safe trips, day or overnight; the latter include stops at wilderness lodges where fishing is said to be phenomenal.

Rocks

The southern beaches are famed for jasper, petrified wood, garnet, and agate. Notable lodes are off the Seven Devils Road north of Bandon, the shore near Gold Beach, and gravel bars of the Rogue River and its tributary, the Illinois River. Fossils are found in cliffs south of Cape Blanco Lighthouse, near Port Orford.

Tourist Information

Brookings Chamber of Commerce, P.O. Box 940, Brookings, OR 97415, (503) 469-2213

Reedsport Chamber of Commerce, Highway 101 & 13th, P.O. Box 356, Reedsport, OR 97467, (503) 271-3495

Seaside Chamber of Commerce, 20 North Columbia, P.O. Box 7, Seaside, OR 98138, (503) 738-6391

Twenty Miracle Miles Chamber of Commerce, 3939 N.W. Highway 101, P.O. Box 797, Lincoln City, OR 97367, (503) 994-3070

Other Information

Campground reservations

Oregon State Parks & Recreation Division, 525 Trade Street S.E., Salem, OR 97310

Phone out-of-state (503) 238-7488

Phone toll free in state 1-800-452-5687

Rogue River tours

Jerry's Rogue River Jet Boats, P.O. Box 1011, Gold Beach, OR 97444, (503) 247-7601

Courts White Water Trips, P.O. Box 1045, Gold Beach, OR 97444, (503) 247-6504 or 247-6676

Rogue Mail Boat Service, P.O. Box 1165, Gold Beach, OR 97444, (503) 247-6225

Reference Books

Exploring the Oregon Coast by Car, by Marje Blood, The Writing Works, 417 E. Pine St., Seattle, WA 98122

Exploring the Seashore, by Gloria Snively, The Writing Works

New Techniques for Catching Bottom Fish, by Doug Wilson & Fred Vander Werff, The Writing Works

Oregon Coast Range Wilderness Trails, Siuslaw Task Force, P.O. Box 863, Corvallis, OR 97330

Oregon Coast Trail Guide Book, Oregon State Parks & Recreation Branch, 525 Trade St. S.E., Salem, OR 97310

Beachcombing the Pacific, by Amos L. Wood, Henry Regnery Co., 180 N. Michigan Ave., Chicago, IL 60601

Beachcombing for Japanese Glass Floats, by Amos L. Wood, Binford & Mort, 2536 S.E. 11th, Portland, OR 97202

Winery Tour

Nehalem Bay Wine Company, Nehalem, OR, (503) 368-5300
Hours: 10 a.m.-5 p.m. daily in summer; noon-5 p.m. in winter

Golf Courses

Warrenton, Astoria Golf and Country Club, 18 holes, private
Gearhart, Gearhart Golf Club, 18 holes, public
Seaside, Seaside Country Club, 9 holes, public
Manzanita, Neah-Kah-Nie Golf Club, 9 holes, public
Tillamook, Alderbrook Country Club, 18 holes, public
Neskowin, Neskowin Golf Club, and Hawk Creek Hills Golf Club, public
Neotsu, Devil's Lake Golf Club, 9 holes, public
Gleneden Beach, Salishan Golf Club, 18 holes, public
Newport, Agate Beach Golf Club, 9 holes, public
Toledo, Olalla Valley Golf Club, 9 holes, public
Waldport, Crestview Hills Golf Club, 9 holes, public
Florence, Rhodo Dunes Golf Club, 9 holes, public
Reedsport, Forest Hills Golf Club, 9 holes, private
North Bend, Kentuck Golf & Country Club, 18 holes, public
Charleston, Sunset Bay Golf Club, 18 holes, public
Coos Bay, Coos Country Club, 9 holes, private
Coquille, Coquille Valley Country Club, 9 holes, public
Bandon, Bandon-Westmost Golf Club, 9 holes, public
Gold Beach, Cedar Bend Golf Club, 9 holes, public

PORTLAND

Oregon

Hub of the Wheel Vacation

The typical large city of modern America sprawls so far over its hinterland that residents and visitors tend to despair of escaping outward for recreation and turn attention inward. Not so with Portland. All the comforts and luxuries of a major city are there. In addition, for a person looking inward, magnificent city parks have fine hiking trails and grand views over the Willamette River and to the snowy volcano of Mt. Hood. But the hinter-

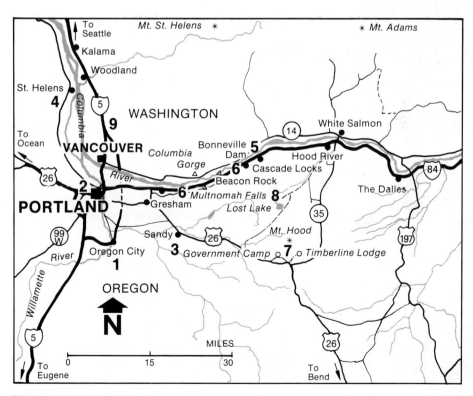

Trillium Lake and Mt. Hood

land is so easy to reach that one can spend a summer day skiing on Hood, dine that evening at a fancy Portland restaurant, and stroll a city park before bedding down in a plush hotel. Next day one can walk an ocean beach and return to the same hotel and that evening take in a movie or play. And next day float down a wild river on a raft, or tour the Columbia Gorge, or hike a meadow in the Cascades, or climb the glaciers of Hood.

Where to Stay

If you're a Hilton, Best Western, or Motel 6 fan, you'll find it in Portland. Every national hotel/motel chain is represented. Other good exploration bases are in motels of the Columbia Gorge.

Near the city are commercial RV/tenter campgrounds. Other campgrounds are operated by Portland General Electric Company. Many more are an hour away in Mt. Hood National Forest.

History

As any loyal Portlander always takes pains to explain, especially to any chauvinistic Seattleite, Portland is an *older* city — in fact, was a genuine city when Seattle was solely inhabited by a band of ragged real estate speculators living on clams while they filed plats in the forest primeval. The Portland area has half again more history than Seattle, and much better preserved.

Fort Vancouver. Just across the Columbia River from the Willamette River settlements that became

Top to bottom: *Pioneer store at Fort Vancouver, parade ground at Fort Vancouver, and logging equipment at the Western Forestry Center*

Portland, Fort Vancouver was founded by the Hudson Bay Company in 1824 and became the hub of commerce in the Northwest. When disputed lands of the Northwest were divided between the United States and Great Britain along the 49th parallel rather than the Columbia, as the company had hoped, it transferred operations north of the new boundary, to a new Vancouver. The old fort became headquarters of the American military during the Indian troubles and was home for several young officers who later became famous generals in the Civil War. In 1949 the fort was placed in the National Park System. The palisade and blockhouse have been rebuilt and locations of other buildings marked. The visitor center depicts history of fort and region. To get there from Portland, drive Interstate 5 north, over the Columbia River, and take the first exit after leaving the bridge. Note the famous apple tree near the exit, planted in 1826.

Oregon City. Dr. John McLoughlin was chief factor of Fort Vancouver and for many years the most respected man in the region, striving to maintain peace between Indians and settlers, missionaries, and Hudson Bay voyageurs. He retired from the company to live in Oregon City, where he built a sawmill next to a waterfall on the Willamette River. The house he built in 1846 is open to the public, daily except Monday, 10 a.m. to 5 p.m. A small fee is charged. After inspecting the house, walk to 7th Street, then toward the river. Cross Singer Hill Road and follow the McLoughlin Promenade along a bluff overlooking the river and a pulp mill. From the promenade a municipal elevator connects the residential area of the upper city to the riverside mills and businesses.

Oregon City from McLoughlin Promenade

French Prairie Loop. A brochure-map published by Oregon State Parks and Recreation Division describes a 40-mile auto tour of French Prairie, in the Willamette Valley just south of Portland. The way passes farms that have been cultivated a century and a half, old homes and barns, the Ox Barn Museum at Aurora, and the townsite of Champoeg, where in 1843 the settlers gathered to form the Oregon Provisional Government.

Portland Walking Tours. Plenty of history is right in Portland. For example, long before any logs were dragged by oxen down Seattle's famous Skid Road, Portland's Burnside was busy and brawling. A great way to learn city history is on the two-hour trips offered by Portland Walking Tours (223-1017); the leader points out the sights and gives a running lecture.

City of Roses

Our focus in this book is the out-of-doors that can be enjoyed *from* the city. The out-of-doors *in* the city, and all the in-doors, we leave to *The*

Portland GuideBook. However, Washington Park is too much for us to pass by without an admiring glance. While we're at it, we'll mention several other trips of different kinds.

Washington Park. No mere "city" park, this, but a vacation in itself, a few blocks from downtown Portland, quickly accessible by Bus No. 63 or by driving Canyon Road (U.S. Highway 26) or West Burnside Street. Picnic area, tennis courts, and the start of a 28-mile foot trail. Forest and views. As is fitting for the City of Roses, there is a world-famous rose test garden, as well as one of the finest collections of rhododendrons in the nation and a Japanese garden. And more besides.

Washington Park Zoo. The best in the Northwest, with more than 400 different animals and birds, including endangered species brought here to breed.

Western Forestry Center. Multi-media exhibits of forest environments, a model sawmill and paper mill, both operating. Forestry

students from Northwest universities come here as part of their classwork.

Oregon Museum of Science and Industry. Study aviation and space exhibits. Converse with a talking machine. Generate electricity with your own pedal power. Light up a love meter. Figure out your chances by the laws of mathematics.

Washington Park and Zoo Railway. For a change of pace, don't drive the mile between zoo and rose garden, take the train.

Pacific Ocean. Just a reminder: all that sand and surf at Cannon Beach is just 80 miles from downtown Portland, and Tillamook is 74 miles, close enough to spend an ocean day sandwiched between days on Mt. Hood and in the Columbia Gorge. See "Oregon Coast."

Sandy River. Parts of the Sandy River, on the outskirts of the city, are safe for beginners to canoe or raft. Both craft can be rented at River Trails, 336 East Columbia Street, Troutdale, OR 97060; (503) 667-1964 or 666-1361. The fee includes a shuttle service for you and the boat—take the float with no worry about how to get back to your car.

Trojan Nuclear Plant. West of Portland (upwind, as nuclear opponents point out) near the town of St. Helens, 40 miles from the city via U.S. Highway 30, is the 499-foot-high cooling tower of the Trojan Nuclear Plant. You can't miss it. A visitor center explains and demonstrates various methods of energy production. A 75-acre wooded recreational park and wildlife sanctuary neighbor the cooling tower and control room, which are open to the public.

Regardless of one's opinion of nuclear power, the tower is an awesome sight. Or as some would say,

Washington Park

Eagle Falls on Eagle Creek

chilling. The citizens of Oregon emphatically said in the elections of 1980 that this probably is the one and only nuclear power plant the state ever will have.

Columbia Gorge

As the Cascade Mountains slowly rose across its path, the Columbia River kept pace, cutting down to maintain a nearly sea level passage from the interior to the ocean. The contest of the eons produced the Columbia Gorge, which might just as well be called Columbia Pass, since it's the lowest point of the Cascade "Crest." As the river carved its way downward in the uprising mountain range, it made vertical cliffs and left slower-cutting tributaries "hanging" in valleys hundreds of feet above the river. From them tumble waterfalls, a series along the gorge, including some of the most spectacular in the Northwest.

There are three ways to see the gorge—by car, by boat, and by boot. For the complete experience try all three.

The Gorge by Car. The full tour, the supreme car trip, is up one side of the gorge, back down the other. The 200 miles could be driven in a day, but there's so much to see that two days are the decent minimum. Motels are conveniently sprinkled along the way and a few campgrounds.

Drive Interstate 84 east from Portland—but don't stay exclusively on freeway, leave it at every exit signed "Scenic Drive," surviving segments of the famous old Columbia Gorge Highway that wound along the cliffs, narrow and slow and magnificent.

The first scenic drive climbs to Crown Point, atop a high bluff with grand views up and down the gorge. Directly below is Rooster Rock State

Columbia River from Crown Point

Park, a very popular place to picnic and swim. It is famous as Oregon's only state park that officially-unofficially permits nature lovers to be totally natural. That is to say, skinny-dipping is allowed at the east end of the park, easily found because that's where most of the cars are parked.

The scenic road winds down the cliffs to river level and Multnomah Falls, a graceful ribbon of water dropping 620 feet in two leaps. Walk the short way to the footbridge over the creek between the two falls. Upstream 2 miles, explore Oneonta Gorge. When the water is low, you can walk right into this narrow slot sliced in hard rock. The scenic road continues upriver to Horsetail Falls and returns to I-84.

Bonneville Dam, first on the Columbia, is a low, run-of-river dam and has an old-fashioned look compared to the high, reservoir-holding, concrete behemoths up the Columbia. Leave I-84 and follow signs through landscaped grounds. Pass the powerhouse and the navigation locks that let barge and boat traffic get by the dam, stop at the visitor center to study the displays and look through the underwater viewing windows to fish climbing the ladders that let them get by the dam. Near the center is the dock from which the tour boat leaves for a two-hour tour up the river.

Return to I-84 but within a mile leave it again for Eagle Creek and hiking trails. Continue to Bridge of the Gods and Cascade Locks National Historic Site, with a visitor center-museum that explains which gods built the bridge and which men built the locks.

Back on I-84 again, reach Hood River—and if your first day is ending, choose from among the excellent motels or the Columbia Gorge Hotel, built in 1921, restored since, and offering a superb view of the river with lovely grounds to wander.

At Hood River you have finished the most spectacular part of the gorge, and most sightseers either cross the Columbia to return to Portland on the Washington side or loop back around Mt. Hood. However, we recommend staying on I-84 another 20 miles to witness the transition from green forests of rain-soaked western Oregon and Washington to sagebrush country in the arid rainshadow of the Cascades. Then cross the Columbia at The Dalles.

The return road down the Washington bank through logging communities is no freeway, but a two-laner with lots of twisting and turning. The highlight is Beacon Rock State Park, pleasant camping and fine hiking on miles of trails. If you've got the head for air, take the "trail" that climbs a series of bridges and stairways to the top of the rock.

The Gorge by Boat. You haven't really seen the gorge until you've seen it from the middle of the Columbia. For a short water tour take the two-hour trip from Bonneville Dam, with a guide who discusses the geology and history.

But the classic river journey is on the *Pacific Northwest Explorer,* an 80-passenger cruise boat that navigates the Columbia and Snake Rivers from Portland to Lewiston, taking nearly a week, passing through eight locks. Guides interpret the passing scene. Stops are frequent at such points and events of interest as Fort Walla Walla, Maryhill, Marmes Shelter, and Indian dances held by the Nez Perce. Any travel agency can book space.

The Gorge Afoot. Short trails along the gorge, to Multnomah Falls and Beacon Rock, already have been mentioned. But there is much more country to walk. Above the highway on slopes of the Oregon Cascades are excellent trails in Mt. Hood National Forest—virgin forests, open meadow slopes with views over the river, and waterfalls the highway traveler never knows exist. There are at least 10 trailheads. Two favorites are the 1½-mile hike from near Horsetail Falls to Oneonta Falls and the 6 miles up Eagle Creek to Eagle Falls.

On the Washington side a trail from the uppermost campsite in Beacon Rock State Park climbs to the 2445-foot summit of Hamilton Mountain and magnificent views. These and other trails will be found on the Forest Service map, "Forest Trails of Columbia Gorge," and in the guidebook, *Hiking Trails in the Columbia Gorge.*

Multnomah Falls

Timberline Lodge and Mt. Hood

Mt. Hood

A common mistake is "doing" the Columbia Gorge and Mt. Hood all in one day. To be sure, the complete loop is an easy six-hour drive. But who goes vacationing to drive? There are too many things to do around Hood to whiz by in a car. The volcano and the gorge can be combined, but allow plenty of time for both. From Portland, drive to Mt. Hood via U.S. Highway 26. From Hood River on Interstate 84, drive State Highway 35 to a junction with U.S. Highway 26 and turn towards Portland. At Timberline Lodge junction turn towards the mountain and climb the road 6 miles to the lodge, in parklands just under 6000 feet.

Timberline Lodge. Critics of New Deal spending whipped themselves into a lather over Timberline Lodge, a project of the WPA and CCC completed in 1937 at a shocking cost of a quarter-million dollars. However, even President Roosevelt's worst enemies had to admit the result was unique. Craftsmen with rare skills in carving wood and working metal and stone were assembled—such a group as could not be found now and could not have been afforded by the public then had it not been for Depression unemployment. Massive beams were squared with broad ax and adze, the marks of the tools plain to see and part of the artistry. Walls were embellished with carvings in the manner of a medieval cathedral. Time has made the lodge even more special, enough to be placed on the National Historic Register.

Here and there the building is showing signs of wear. The U.S. Forest Service estimates more than 30 million people have walked through the entry onto the oak floors. That's 60 million feet on the floors and probably 150 million fingers caressing the carvings along the stairways. The Forest Service is supervising restoration work.

The lodge is open year-around. For a special treat spend the night.

Skiing. Summer and winter the Palmer Chairlift carries skiers up the Palmer Snowfield, a permanent snowfield between the Zigzag and White River Glaciers. If you feel foolish driving around in August with skis on your car, they can be rented at the lodge.

Hiking. The most exciting views of the 11,235-foot volcano, its glaciers and lava ramparts, are from trails. Those lower on the mountain, in forests, are usually snow-free from mid-June when the rhododendrons are in bloom. The higher trails may be snowy until late July when the alpine flower show ordinarily climaxes.

The Timberline Trail, a 40-mile, up-and-down, around-the-mountain route, is a Northwest classic, through valley-bottom forests with rhododendrons taller than a basketball player and highland meadows bright with blossoms and a thousand different perspectives on the volcano. The hike is safe for any knowledgeable hiker if he takes care not to lose the way in lingering snow patches, and keeps in mind that low clouds moving toward the mountain or wisps of fog materializing out of nowhere can mean a sudden fogstorm that whites out the world.

Our favorite hike is on the Timberline Trail 4½ miles west from Timberline Lodge to flower fields of Paradise Park. The elevation is about the same on both ends but in between are lots of ups and downs.

At arms-length distance from Hood, Lost Lake Butte, a former lookout site, gives a feeling for the full scale of the peak.

The Pacific Crest Trail extends north from Hood to Canada and south to Mexico. For any of these trails you will need a Mt. Hood National Forest map.

Climbing. A thousand or more people climb the mountain each year, mainly in the period from May, after avalanche hazard lessens, to mid-July, before the rockfall gets too intense. Most of the way is simply a long, strenuous walk but the upper 1500 feet skirt crevasses and ascend very steep snow. Unless you know climbing or have an experienced leader, don't try it on your own.

However, the professional guides of Lute Jerstad Adventures can equip you and take you to the top safely and comfortably. Lute, one of the Americans who climbed Everest in 1963, also conducts four-day ice-climbing seminars on the north side of Hood.

Climbers on Eliot Glacier, Mt. Hood

Mt. St. Helens

Chances are the Number One tourist attraction of the Northwest for the next few years will be the only active (and how!) volcano in the 48 conterminous states. People are flocking from all over the world, hoping to get ashed. Portland is getting rather blasé, what with eruption alerts and ashfalls as common as blizzards in North Dakota or hurricanes in Florida. The volcano is prominently seen from

Mt. St. Helens erupting, 1980

many places around the city — when ash clouds don't block the view.

In this First Year of St. Helens the only way to gain any notion of what happened in the immediate vicinity is to buy a book of photographs (dozens are in the bookstores) or see a movie (dozens are around). The closest experience for the average tourist is at the Mt. St. Helens Information Center of the U.S. Forest Service with photos, movies, and interpretive displays. Drive Interstate 5 north past Vancouver, Washington, to Exit 14 and follow signs.

If and when the volcano calms down, closer approaches will be permitted. Already an experienced hiker can find trails to awesome views — but nothing compared to those routinely offered by photographers flying over and putting on a show on the evening TV news. At last count approximately 138,000 Northwest shops will sell you a bag of St. Helens ash — but you can gather your own, there are billions of tons all over Oregon and Washington, free for the taking.

Note: Mt. Hood has been stirring recently, making people nervous. Within the city of Portland is an extinct volcano, Mt. Tabor. At least, everybody *hopes* it's extinct.

Tourist Information

Visitors Information Center, Portland Chamber of Commerce, 824 S.W. Fifth Ave., Portland, OR 97204, (503) 228-9411

Other Information

U.S. Forest Service information and maps:

U.S. Forest Service, Regional Office, 319 S.W. Pine St., (P.O. Box 3623), Portland, OR 97208, (503) 221-2877

Maps:

Mt. Hood National Forest, 50c

Forest Trails of Columbia Gorge, 50c

Ask for free list of all Forest Service maps

Mountain climbing guide:

Lute Jerstad Adventures, Inc., P.O. Box 19527, Portland, OR 97219, (503) 244-4364

Walking tours:

Portland Walking Tours, P.O. Box 4322, Portland, OR 97208, (503) 223-1017

Hiking and climbing rentals and sales and USGS maps:

R.E.I. (Recreational Equipment, Inc.), 1798 Jantzen Beach Center, Portland, OR, (503) 283-1300

Reference Books

The Portland GuideBook, by Linda Lampman & Julie Sterling, The Writing Works, 417 E. Pine St., Seattle, WA 98122

Portland Super Shopper, by Connie & Terry Hofferber, The Writing Works

Winery Tours, by Tom Stockley, The Writing Works

62 Hiking Trails–Northern Oregon Cascades, by Don & Roberta Lowe, The Touchstone Press, P.O. Box 81, Beaverton, OR 97005

Hiking Trails in the Columbia Gorge, by Oral Bullard & Don Lowe, The Touchstone Press

A Guide to the Trails of Badger Creek, by Ken & Ruth Love, Signpost Books, 8912 192nd S.W., Edmonds, WA 98020

Winery Tours

Henry Endres Winery, 13300 S. Clackamas River Drive, Oregon City, OR, (503) 656-7239, Hours: 11 a.m.-7 p.m. Tues.-Sat.

Mt. Hood Winery, Woodworth Road, Mt. Hood, OR, (503) 352-3645, Hours: 1-5 p.m. Tues.-Sun.

Oak Knoll Winery, Burkhalter Road, Hillsboro, OR, (503) 648-8198, Hours: 2-6 p.m. Thurs. & Sun.; 11 a.m.-6 p.m. Sat.

Golf Courses in Portland

Broadmoor Golf Club, 18 holes, public
Columbia-Edgewater Country Club, 18 holes, private
Colwood Golf Club, 18 holes, public
Eastmoreland Golf Club, 18 holes, public
Glendoveer Golf Club, 36 holes, public
Portland Golf Club, 18 holes, private
Portland Meadows Golf Club, 9 holes, public
Riverside Golf & Country Club, 18 holes, private
Rose City Golf Club, 18 holes, public
Top O'Scott Golf Club, 18 holes, public
Waverley Country Club, 18 holes, private
West Delta Park Golf Club, 18 holes, public

UPPER WILLAMETTE VALLEY

Oregon

Hub of the Wheel Vacation

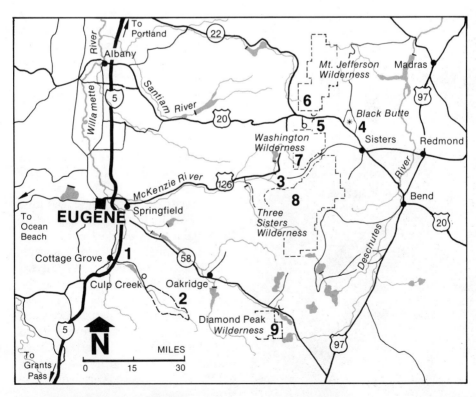

Lundberg Stage House at Musick Mine

Upper Willamette Valley

T he Willamette Valley is deceptive. Mostly flat and gently rolling, broad and greenly pastoral it seems a peaceful spot to live but scarcely an exciting place to vacation, unless bicycling quiet farm lanes is your sport, pausing to soak up scenery and history (and what's boring about that?). However, just a short drive east is the Cascade Range, with five wilderness areas and hundreds of miles of trails, plus ghost towns. From the mountains flow rivers wonderful to raft, great to fish. And west of the valley, just a short drive over the Oregon Coast Range, is the Pacific Ocean.

Deady Hall, built 1872, at University of Oregon, Eugene

Where to Stay

The twin cities of Eugene and Springfield are logical headquarters, offering motels and hotels of every degree of simplicity and luxury, restaurants to match, and cultural resources generated by the presence of the University of Oregon.

To be lulled to sleep by babbling waters, try a motel or lodge up the McKenzie River.

For campers, just north of Eugene is Armitage State Park, with a few tent sites but no facilities for RVs—which, however, can find space at commercial operations. To the east in Willamette National Forest are numerous campgrounds on rivers and reservoirs.

History

In the 1950s, when easy-to-cut virgin forests were getting scarce in Washington, the timber industry shifted major attention to central Oregon. Lane County became the logging capital of the West, and Eugene mushroomed from a relaxed university-and-farm town to Oregon's second city. However, the valley past is well-preserved, and it's long and fascinating, extending to the 1850s and beyond.

Historic Buildings. Detailed maps of old buildings are supplied by the Eugene and Cottage Grove Chambers of Commerce. The oldest surviving structure is the County Clerk's Office, built in 1853 and now on the Lane County Fairgrounds. Still in use on the University of Oregon campus are Deady Hall, 1872, and Villard Hall, 1885. Buildings in Cottage Grove dating from the turn of the century exhibit well-preserved period architecture.

Mosby Creek Bridge built in 1920 near Cottage Grove

Oregon-Pacific Railroad. This is a working railroad that hauls forest products 35 miles from mills at Culp Creek down the Row River to Cottage Grove. However, there also is a passenger train, during the week leaving daily at 2 p.m., July 1 through Labor Day, pulled by a diesel locomotive.

Weekends are the special treat. At 10 a.m. and 2 p.m., the *Goose*, a 1914 steam engine, chugs out of the station, hauling the passenger cars behind.

Covered Bridges. In the East bridges were covered so they wouldn't collapse under winter snows. Why they were built in rain country is a mystery to me—perhaps because the builders came from the East and felt a bridge looked naked without a hat. In any event, Lane County has 21 covered bridges, probably more than the combined total everywhere else in the West.

The first was built in 1920, the most recent in 1966. The oldest, Mosby Creek Bridge, is just east of Cottage Grove. Take Mosby Creek Road and in a couple miles turn right on Row River Road to the bridge. A bit farther on is the Currin Bridge built in 1925. Best-known is Goodpasture Bridge, built over the McKenzie River in 1938. Spot it beside the McKenzie Pass Highway near Vida.

Bohemia Mining Area. In 1858 gold was found in the Calapooya Mountains, a western spur of the Cascades. The first strike, named after a James Johnson, nicknamed "Bohemia," didn't amount to much, but in 1863 two prospectors spotted yellow glitterings in quartz and the gold rush began. It's never really stopped, the fever falls and rises— a whole new delirium was set off in the late 1970s by $600-an-ounce-gold.

Whether or not mining relics are your taste, the views are worth the

Entrance to Musick Mine. The mine shaft has partly collapsed.

tour, and in late June and early July an added attraction is the mass blooming of rhododendron and beargrass. But be warned: the road is very steep and, if the grader hasn't been along recently, can be too rocky for a standard passenger car. Ask about road conditions and alternate roads at the Row River Ranger Station, a short distance out of Cottage Grove. There or from the Cottage Grove Chamber of Commerce buy the brochure, *Tour of the Golden Past,* describing the trip and telling the history.

The highlight is the Musick Mine, where buildings are being restored by the Cottage Grove Prospectors' Club. Get there via a short sideroad about a mile beyond Bohemia Saddle.

For scenery visit 5933-foot Fairview Peak, with views from the Willamette Valley to volcanoes of the Cascade Crest. In early summer the slopes below the fire lookout on the summit are brilliant with wildflowers. Find the road at Bohemia Saddle. The last quarter-mile is a four-wheel drive road, so park and walk.

Scouting Around by Car: McKenzie Pass Loop

From Willamette Valley to High Lava Plateau and back again, crossing and recrossing the Cascades, this 200-mile loop can be driven in five hours—if one is blind to virgin forests, pretty sparkling rivers, alpine lakes, and massive volcanoes. If the eyes are open, however, two days are a minimum, stopping overnight at one of the numerous campgrounds or motels or at a flossy resort near Sisters, the halfway point. Note: You can't do the loop towing a trailer—McKenzie Pass is out of bounds for unwieldy rigs.

Drive State Highway 126 east from Eugene-Springfield, following the McKenzie River upstream. At Blue River enter virgin forest dominated by Douglas fir several hundred feet high, 4 to 6 feet in diameter. To see impressive specimens, visit Paradise Campground.

At Foley Springs keep right on State Highway 242 and climb through forest, then stark lava surrounding Belknap Crater, to McKenzie Pass, 5324 feet. Visit the observatory for an explanation of the lava, which appears as if it might still be hot but actually cooled 2000 years ago. The observatory has pointers identifying the peaks, including Mt. Washington to the north and North Sister to the south. To grasp the magnitude of the fields of frozen magma, walk at least a little way north on the Pacific Crest Trail. Better, hike on 2 miles up Little Belknap Crater to look at fissures, tunnels, and spatter cones.

From the pass descend to beautiful forests of ponderosa pine. Perhaps stop overnight at Sisters, 92 miles from Eugene, well-supplied with motels and resorts, including Rock Springs Guest Ranch, which looks very expensive. Turn west again on U.S. Highway 20 (State 126).

For a spectacular view of volcanic peaks, hike to the fire lookout atop 6436-foot Black Butte. From north to south you'll see Hood, Jefferson, Three Fingered Jack, Washington, North Sister, South Sister, and Broken Top. Only Middle Sister, hidden behind North Sister, is missing. To get there, drive 6 miles west from Sisters on Highway 20/126 and turn north on Forest Service Road 1139,

Big Lake and Mt. Washington

signed "Green Ridge." Between 3 and 4 miles turn left on Forest Service Road 1318, signed "Black Butte Trail," and follow it 5 miles to the end. The 2-mile trail, gaining about 1400 feet, can get warm and has no water, so carry some. Aside from views there is history—the original lookout still stands with a cupola tower, built sometime between 1920-25. Once there were a hundred or more lookouts of this design, but now only three are left in Oregon and one in Washington; this surely deserves to be a national historic building. More recently, an 85-foot lookout tower was constructed which wobbles a bit in the breeze, as exciting as the volcanoes.

Return to Highway 20/126 and climb to 4817-foot Santiam Pass. On the west side turn south on a paved

Lookout on 85-foot tower and old lookout building on Black Butte

Alton Baker Park, Eugene

road to Big Lake Campground and a fine view of Mt. Washington. On the way see Three Fingered Jack. (Beside the road we watched five deer browsing.)

At 6 miles from Santiam Pass keep left on Highway 20/126 and in another 4 miles keep left again, on State Highway 126. It's all downhill, through lava from Belknap Crater and some of the finest virgin forest remaining in the nation, and then back to Eugene-Springfield.

Bicycling

There may be more bicycles per capita in Lane County than anywhere in the West, and why not? The city has miles of specially-marked bicycle lanes and bike paths along both sides of the Willamette River, connected by two motor-free bridges, and 4 miles of bike trails in Alton Baker Park. Plus all those backroads through the farmlands. For rentals see the Yellow Pages.

Reservoiring-Fishing

Lane County might well be called "Lake County"—or more accurately, "Reservoir County." Within an hour's drive of Eugene-Springfield are 10 dams-reservoirs built by the Army Corps of Engineers: Cougar, Fall Creek, Lookout Point, Dexter, Dorena, Fern Ridge, Hills Creek, Green Peter, Foster, and Blue River—all called "lakes." Each offers camping, boating, and—primarily—fishing. For reservoir maps write Portland District Corps of Engineers, P.O. Box 2946, Portland, OR 97208.

Boats can be rented at reservoir resorts. With or without a boat, fishing is good; check with a local sporting goods store to find out where they're biting at the moment.

River Rafting-Fishing

You also can fish from a raft, or raft just to enjoy the float, or combine pleasures. If inexperienced in whitewater rafting, you need help. The

Eugene Chamber of Commerce has a brochure listing fishing-rafting guide services, which in the Yellow Pages number a dozen or more. Reservations are necessary for overnight trips but often not for day floats.

The McKenzie River is great for beginners. The popular day run is 14 miles down from Blue River, mostly smooth water but with enough rapids to take your breath away. If you hunger for more thrills, the guides will take you higher on the river or on two-day trips down the North Umpqua. If you then are hooked on floating, they'll be happy to lead you to the Snake River and Rogue River, discussed in other vacations.

Hot Springs

If you belong to that cult that devoutly worships hot water coming out of the ground, you have three shrines here, two developed and one primitive.

Belknap Hot Springs. A resort with swimming pool, cabins, and camping, (503) 822-3535.

Breitenbush Hot Springs. A resort with bathhouse, cabins, and camping.

Cougar   Reservoir   Hot

Rafting on the McKenzie River

Springs. A small pool in the National Forest, reached by a ½-mile trail from the road on the west side of Cougar Reservoir.

Ocean

Just a reminder: Eugene is a quick 60 miles via State Highway 126 from the beaches at Florence, close enough for the vacation day to be spent mostly in the sand, not on the road— and close enough for a spur-of-the-moment picnic supper to watch the sunset. See "Oregon Coast."

Hiking

The Upper Willamette Valley is a hotbed not only of bicycling but of hiking. In the Coast Range are paths minutes from the cities, and beaches of the (to-be) Oregon Coast Trail are a bit more than an hour away. In the broad expanse of the Western Cascades are fine trails along the McKenzie River and Middle Fork Willamette River. Understandably the High Cascades

Fishing in the McKenzie River

A quiet stretch of the McKenzie River

Mt. Jefferson

are the best-known. There, strung
along the Pacific Crest National Scenic
Trail, are no less than four National
Wilderness Areas. Only a few hints
can be tossed out here as to what nice
things await the hiker. For detailed
guidance buy the guidebooks, *Pacific
Crest Trail, Volume 2,* and *60 Hiking
Trails, Central Oregon Cascades.* Before starting out, it would be best to get
a Willamette National Forest map and
the appropriate wilderness map.

Northernmost is Mt. Jefferson
Wilderness, north of Santiam Pass. In
5 miles from the pass the Crest Trail
traverses slopes of 7841-foot Three
Fingered Jack and at 24 miles reaches

Pamelia Lake on the side of glacier-
white Jefferson, 10,497 feet. Another
trail leaves the road a mile west of
Santiam Pass and goes 8 miles to
Eight Lakes Basin.

South of Santiam lies Mt.
Washington Wilderness, a chaos of
broken lava, forbidding but fascinating.

South of McKenzie Pass are
Three Sisters Wilderness and French
Pete Wilderness—a single unit, really, though it took years for conserva-
tionists to save the latter from the loggers who lusted after its noble forests.
A whole generation became battle-
hardened in this controversy and went

on to fight in other campaigns. The hiking is some of the finest in Oregon. For a sample, hike south from 5324-foot McKenzie Pass on the Crest Trail, skirting lava beds, and in 2½ miles lose 300 feet to North Matthew Lake. The way then climbs above timberline and at 8 miles from the road comes to 6400-foot Oppie Dildock Pass and a view of the Collier Glacier between North and Middle Sisters. It then rounds all Three Sisters and within a stone's throw passes a hundred lakes or lakelets; for a quicker way to the lakes, see "Bend." Don't expect solitude on the Crest Trail or at the lakes. For that, try the forests of French Pete.

Diamond Peak Wilderness is quite small, has comparatively little mountains, few lakes, not many hikers, and a good chance to be lonesome.

Wilderness permits are required to camp in the wilderness areas. They are free at any ranger station.

Tourist Information

Cottage Grove Chamber of Commerce 1785 E. Main Street, P.O. Box 587, Cottage Grove, OR 97424, (503) 942-2411

Eugene-Springfield Convention and Visitors Bureau, Inc., 1401 Willamette St., P.O. Box 10286, Eugene, OR 97440, (503) 484-5307

Other Information

U.S. Forest Service information and maps:

Williamette National Forest, 211 E. 7th Ave., (P.O. Box 10607), Eugene, OR 97401, (503) 687-6522

Maps

Willamette National Forest, 50c
Mt. Jefferson Wilderness, 50c
Mt. Washington Wilderness, 50c
Three Sisters Wilderness, 50c

U.S. Army Corps of Engineers maps:

Portland District, Corps of Engineers, P.O. Box 2946, Portland, OR 97208

Reference Books

60 Hiking Trails, Central Oregon Cascades, by Don & Roberta Lowe, The Touchstone Press, P.O. Box 81, Beaverton, OR 97005

Pacific Crest Trail, Vol. 2: Oregon and Washington, Wilderness Press, 2440 Bancroft Way, Berkeley, CA 94704

Golf Courses

Eugene
   Eugene Country Club, 18 holes, private
   Green Acres Golf Club, 18 holes, public
   Laurelwood Country Club, 9 holes, public
   Oakway Golf Club, 18 holes, public

Springfield
   Springfield Country Club, 9 holes, private

ROGUE RIVER

Oregon

Hub of the Wheel Vacation

W hat a combination! Spend the day fighting rapids of the Rogue River and that evening attend a Shakespeare play performed by the finest company in America and staged in an authentic Elizabethan theater. Climb Shasta, one of the nation's tallest peaks, and on the way back admire redwoods, the world's tallest trees. Walk ocean beaches, walk alpine meadows, walk around Crater Lake, and walk underground in the Oregon Caves. If that's not enough, poke around a town founded by gold rushers just three years after the big strike in California.

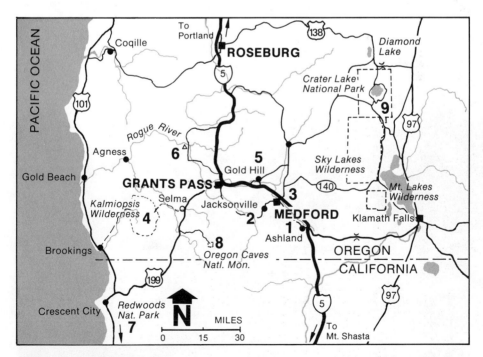

Rafting the Wild Rogue River

Where to Stay

Grants Pass, Medford, and Ashland have motels and inns ranging from deluxe with swimming pools and color TV to plain and simple for a skinny budget. The Jacksonville Inn, built in 1863, has eight rooms restored in antique furnishings; by modern standards it may not be the lap of luxury, but sleep there and you may dream about cowboys and Indians, Civil War generals, or Queen Victoria.

A resort on Howard Prairie Reservoir offers facilities for RVs and tents; it also rents trailers. The Last Resort, on Lake Selmac, west of Grants Pass on U.S. Highway 199, has a campground for tents and trailers (but no cabins) and boats and canoes to rent; the bicycling around the lake is fun.

Within 20 miles of the triplet cities are many campgrounds—a KOA, two state parks, five county parks, and others.

Drama and Music

How did it happen that the nation's most famous Shakespearean theater, shrine of fans of the bard from around the world, is located in a sleepy little town in the Siskiyou Mountains of southern Oregon? Credit the chance circumstances that brought here, half a century ago, Angus Bowmer, an English teacher with a big idea. Credit, too, the community response to his idea, its participation since 1935 in the festival he founded. As recently as 20 years ago only a comparative handful of initiates made the annual summer pilgrimage to the outdoor theater, replica of one in which Shakespeare's own company performed. The skill of the staging, the quality of the acting, and the charms of the setting amid forests and mountains now draw throngs from afar.

Indeed, the throngs are such that to be sure of seeing the plays you want—or any plays at all—tickets

Shakespearean Theater, Ashland

United States Hotel built in 1880 at Jacksonville

are best bought months ahead. For a play schedule write Oregon Shakespearean Festival, Ashland, OR 97520, or call (503) 482-4331. Your travel agent may also have a schedule.

In addition to the Elizabethan Theater two indoor theaters perform everything from Shakespeare to O'Casey to contemporary works.

Summer evenings hereabouts are very esthetic. The **Peter Britt Music Festival,** held annually in August, presents concerts under the stars featuring some of the nation's finest musicians. For the schedule write P.O. Box 1124, Medford, OR 97501.

History: Jacksonville

"Gold! Gold! There's gold in Oregon!"

With scarcely a pause to draw breath after the rush west to California, in 1851 the '49ers rushed north. A week after the first strike an empty corner of the mountains became the bustling settlement of Jacksonville, ever since the center of the region's history.

When the gold ran out, Jacksonville was not abandoned. It's very lively still, yet takes pains to preserve buildings that are among Oregon's oldest. The courthouse, built in 1883

Bear Creek Bicycle and Nature Trail in Medford

when this was the county seat, is now a museum. The railroad station built in 1891 is occupied by the Chamber of Commerce. On California Street is the U.S. Hotel, 1880. Next door is the Beekman Bank Building, 1863. Down the street is the Methodist Church, 1854. Some old buildings house specialty shops. Many old homes are homes yet. Britt Gardens, founded in 1852 by Peter Britt, pioneer photographer and horticulturist, are the scene in August of the Britt Music Festival.

Just outside town is Pioneer Village, a commercial museum. Wagons and buggies are displayed, and mining equipment, and 20 buildings of the 19th century that have been moved here from elsewhere in the vicinity.

The most direct route to Jacksonville, 5 miles from Interstate 5, is from Medford via State Highway 238. However, the road from Grants Pass and the old stagecoach road are more interesting.

Bicycling

Medford is beloved of bicyclists for its Bear Creek Nature and Bicycling National Recreation Trail, which is even longer than its name. The paved walkway-bikeway follows banks of Bear Creek through town.

Back roads around Medford are quiet and scenic, fine biking. The road to Jacksonville, though tourist-busy, also is popular.

Bicycles can be rented at Siskiyou Cyclery, 1259 Siskiyou Boulevard, Medford; phone, (503) 482-1997.

Rogue River

Under the National Wild and Scenic Rivers Act of 1968, 84 miles of the Rogue, plus an average of a quarter-mile of land on either side, have been classified as "wild river" or "scenic river" or "recreational river," to protect the natural beauty. Decades before river-running became a national fad sport, boats were as plentiful on the Rogue as fish in it; if any river in the country is more popular we don't know it. Many and varied are the craft that ply the waters. And on the riverbank are boots.

Motoring and Fishing the Rogue. Powerboats are permitted without restriction on stretches of the river designated Scenic or Recreational, as well as on those without federal protection. Outboard motors are common in the Grants Pass vicinity, popular with fishermen who drift downstream and motor back; rentals are available at resorts near Grants Pass.

Jet-propelled "mailboats" run on a regular schedule from Gold Beach, on the ocean shore, upstream 32 miles to Agness, a 6-hour round trip, safe and comfortable. A longer trip continues another 20 miles upstream into Wild (not quite) River, serving commercial lodges. For more about Gold Beach trips see "Oregon Coast."

Rafting for Beginners. The Rogue is the favorite rafting river in the West. Much of the way is strictly for experts but the waters between Grants Pass and Medford are easy enough for beginners. No river is abso-

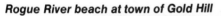
Rogue River beach at town of Gold Hill

Easy rafting on the Rogue River near Gold Hill

lutely safe but with proper equipment and common sense anyone can enjoy the floating, swimming, sunbathing, and fishing here.

Drive to Gold Hill a half-mile off I-5 between Grants Pass and Medford. Near the big bridge is Jay's Raft Trips, which will rent you a raft and safety gear and pick up you and the raft after the float and return you to the starting point.

Drifting the Wild Rogue. Permits are required to drift the Wild Rogue; the U.S. Forest Service limits the number of people at any one time to the number of spaces in campsites (and lodges) along the way. Thousands of requests come in annually—more than can be granted, so make your reservation well in advance with the Forest Service in Grants Pass.

Campgrounds are conveniently spaced. The lodges—located on private inholdings—will take drop-in customers, but by reservation only.

Turbulent with boiling eddies, violent currents, and powerful waves, much of the Rogue—the crowd-drawing part—is purely for those with white-water experience. If you don't have enough, or any, sign up with a competent guide. A list of the 43 guide services licensed for the Rogue can be obtained from the U.S. Forest Service in Grants Pass, and a brochure giving their prices from the Grants Pass Chamber of Commerce. Be sure to get the Forest Service map, *The Wild Rogue.*

The 32 miles of the Rogue from Grants Pass to Graves Creek Bridge are partly unclassified, partly (below Applegate River) Recreational River, a status reflecting the fact that roads are close along the banks. The water begins easy but becomes somewhat more turbulent. Canoers and kayakers love it. Motorboats are permitted and common. The number of users is not limited. Stopovers can be made at several resorts and county parks on the banks.

At Graves Creek Bridge commences Wild River. The waters from here 33 miles down to Big Bend are rated moderate, difficult, and extremely difficult. Squeezed in a narrow canyon, the river alternates between calm pools and violent rapids. Except for those serving lodges, powerboats are not permitted. Kayaks and canoes are not recommended. The usual craft are rafts and McKenzie River drift boats. Entry and camping are by Forest Service permit only. Most people make the trip with a guide.

Below Big Bend is Recreational River to Agness, then Scenic River, Recreational again to the mouth of Lobster Creek, below which the river is unclassified. The waters are easy, the powerboats many, and civilization near.

Hiking the Rogue. Which is most exciting, rafting the Wild Rogue or hiking it? To each his own. For some the rafting is too exciting. Admiring the water from shore is fun enough. The trail lies partly at water's edge, partly high above with sweeping views. The canyon is an oven by the middle of the day, very sweaty for exercise. The best plan is to hike in early morning, spend the afternoon fishing and swimming, and perhaps walk some more in the cool of evening.

A permit must be obtained from the Forest Service in Grants Pass, but there is no limit on the number of hikers.

Rafting the Wild Rogue River with expert guides

Redwood National Park

Cathedrals of ancient trees 2000 years old, the tallest on earth. Aisles through rhododendrons billowing high above your head. A forest floor carpeted with ferns and flowers. A fit place to worship.

Jedediah Smith Redwoods State Park, 75 miles southwest of Grants Pass on U.S. Highway 199, is the northernmost link in a 50-mile chain of three state parks and several segments of Redwood National Park. Here is the Stout Tree, the largest (though not the tallest) redwood, 20 feet in diameter and 340 feet high. The highway is a tunnel through towering trees but the viewing is less machine-hectic on the tour road and better yet on the trail. One trail leads to the world's tallest tree, 368 feet.

There also are miles of ocean beach, with bays and rocks where brown pelicans and sea lions can be seen. In the forest are elk that never have been hunted and thus don't run away from cameras.

Left: *Redwoods in Redwood National Park*

Bottom: *Oxalis carpeting the forest floor*

To tour the whole park plan to spend two to three days, staying in a motel at Crescent City or camping in any of the state parks. Maps are supplied at the state parks and at the National Park headquarters in Crescent City. No problem finding the headquarters—the way is well marked and the building arches across a city street.

Oregon Caves National Monument

A half-mile-long cave carved from marble by water. The 1¼-hour walk is partly in large chambers, partly a squeeze through narrow defiles. The way is lighted and has handrails where needed.

Drive west on U.S. Highway 199 to Cave Junction, 30 miles west of Grants Pass; motels and a state park provide a base. Take State Highway 46

another 20 miles to the caves. The last 8 miles are narrow and steep, though paved, ending in a parking lot with limited space. During the peak of the season you'd better arrive early, or you may have a long wait in line just to park.

The cave walk must be done with a guide. No children under six are allowed (there is a baby-sitting service), and people with breathing, heart, or walking problems should stay out. Guides and baby-sitting are provided by the concessionaire. Buy your ticket as soon as you arrive; if there's a long wait for a guide, hike one of the forest trails from the lot until it's your turn for the tour.

Food and lodging are available near the cave entrance at the Chateau, a hotel rustic on the outside, modern on the inside.

Oregon Caves National Monument

Crater Lake Loop

In 1980, Mt. St. Helens blew one cubic kilometer of itself into the sky. Mt. Mazama, 6600 years ago, blew out 42 cubic kilometers. People in central Washington had a bad day, that recent May 18th. How do you suppose the central-Oregon Indians of long ago liked *their* show? A 200-mile round-trip drive from Medford goes through miles of lovely forest beside the Rogue River and climaxes at Crater Lake, in the heart of what's left of Mazama.

Drive State Highway 62 north past Shady Cove and Lost Creek Reservoir into Rogue River National Forest. Turn left on State Highway 230. The road climbs from one forest type to another, lowland species of trees yielding to the highland. The road cuts through banks of yellow pumice blown out in the cataclysm; note the black roots and logs sticking out of the banks, remnants of trees buried in the ash.

Highway 230 ends at a junction with State Highway 138. To the left 3

Deer in Oregon Caves National Monument

miles is Diamond Lake, with campgrounds, a resort, rental boats, and a dramatic view of another volcano fragment, 9182-foot Thielsen. To the right is Crater Lake National Park. Pick up a brochure when entering the park and drive to the caldera rim for views. For more about the park see "Klamath."

To complete the loop, leave the park at the south entrance and return to Medford on State Highway 62.

Hiking and Climbing

Three mountain ranges—the Cascades, the Coast Range, and the link connecting them, the Siskiyous —attract the boots in all directions. Most of the trail country is discussed in following sections on the Rogue River, Redwood National Park, Oregon Caves National Monument, and Crater Lake National Park. However, several other areas compete for attention.

On the Cascade Crest is Sky Lakes Wilderness, described in the Klamath vacation. From Medford drive north on State Highway 62, then east on State Highway 140 to Lake of the Woods.

In the Coast Range is Kalmiopsis Wilderness, with hot hillsides in summer, but delightful and cool river bottoms and everywhere lonesome. To find trailheads, obtain a Siskiyou National Forest map at the headquarters in Grants Pass. Access from Grants Pass is via U.S. Highway 199, then down the Illinois River to forest roads to the wilderness boundary.

If climbing's your game and 14,161-foot Shasta your aim, the monster volcano is only 40 miles south on I-5. Do it on your own if you know how; for climbing lessons or a summit guide, call High Chalet in Klamath

Falls, (503) 884-3285, as noted in "Klamath."

Speaking of pedestrian sport, don't ignore Lithia Park, right in Ashland. You'll not soon forget an evening that begins with an after-dinner stroll on forest paths through the cool canyon past ponds and mineral-water fountains and ends with a few steps to the next-door Elizabethan Theater to hear blank verse under the sky of the summer night.

Tourist Information

Ashland Chamber of Commerce, 110 E. Main St., P.O. Box 606, Ashland, OR 97520, (503) 482-3486

Grants Pass Chamber of Commerce, 1439 N.E. 6th St., P.O. Box 970, Grants Pass, OR 97526, (503) 476-7717

Medford Chamber of Commerce, 304 S. Central, Medford, OR 97501, (503) 772-6293

Other Information

U.S. Forest Service information, maps, and river permits:

Siskiyou National Forest, 1504 N.W. 6th St., (P.O. Box 440), Grants Pass, OR 97526, (503) 479-5301

Maps

Siskiyou National Forest, 50c
Rogue River National Forest 50c
Kalmiopsis Wilderness/Wild Rogue Wilderness, 50c
The Wild and Scenic Rogue River, free in 1980

Theater

Oregon Shakespearean Festival, Ashland, OR 97520, (503) 482-4331

Reference Book

Winery Tours, by Tom Stockley, The Writing Works, 417 E. Pine St., Seattle, WA 98122

Winery Tour

Valley View Winery, 1352 Applegate Road, Jacksonville, Or 97530, (503) 899-8896
Hours: Weekends, but owners suggest visitors call ahead

Golf Courses

Ashland
Oak Knoll Golf Club, 9 holes, public
Grants Pass
Colonial Valley Golf Club, 9 holes, public
Grants Pass Country Club, 18 holes, public
Medford
Cedar Links Golf Club, 9 holes, public
Rogue Valley Country Club, 27 holes, private
Roxy Ann Links, 9 holes, public

BEND

Oregon

Hub of the Wheel Vacation

Visitors are drawn to Bend by the most varied array of volcanic features in the United States outside Hawaii. They come, too, for the wilderness trails winding through forests and meadows to mountain lakes and high summits. Others are attracted by the largest assemblage of ospreys in the conterminous 48 states, or the river-running, the fishing, the summer-long skiing, the bicycling, the scenic drives and idyllic campsites, or the cushy re-

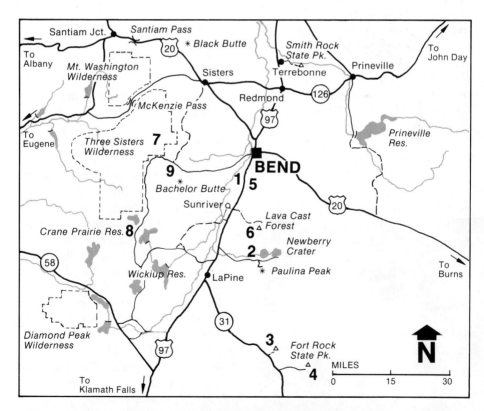

Osprey feeding on a fish near Crane Prairie Reservoir

sorts designed to exploit the "high desert" climate—day after day of blue sky and sunshine, yet, due to the altitude, rarely any uncomfortable heat.

Bend

Bend—orginially called Farewell Bend because there, at a turn in the Deschutes River, the emigrant route left the stream—is about as pleasant a spot as could be found for a city. Its elevation is 3628 feet, exactly at the meeting place of two geological provinces, the High Cascades and the High Lava Plain. The population of 18,000 is enough to support all the basic services and amenities a vacationer might wish. In addition, as a long-time major travelers' stopover, the city overflows with motels and restaurants. Most are along U.S. Highway 97. The old city lies to the west, with handsome brick buildings and lovely parks on banks of the river.

In the city are two places a visitor must not miss. Pilot Butte, a cinder cone rising 500 feet from the plain on the outskirts of town, was so named because it "piloted" pioneers from afar. Prominent from a great distance, it gives views to a great distance. To get there drive Greenwood Avenue (U.S.

Highway 20) from downtown to the foot of the butte, then shift into low gear for the final steep bit to the summit. Gaze around the compass: to the east sprawl ranches and forests and sagebrush prairies of the High Lava Plain. To the west, in a row, are vents of the Pacific Rim of Fire, snowcapped volcanoes extending north into Washington, south into California.

From Bend's high point descend to its low, the city park along the Deschutes River. Sit in the grass and watch ducks float and fish swim through cool shadows of willows overhanging the limeade stream.

Where to Stay

Near Bend in Deschutes National Forest are more than 30 developed campgrounds, some in pine forests, others by lakes. For a complete list write to Lava Lands Visitor Center, Bend, OR 97701.

Many car-campers prefer the undeveloped campsites scattered along forest roads. Facilities are primitive, but the solitude and quiet reward the roughing-it.

Even hikers and campers often enjoy a night in a motel to wash off grime and let mosquito bites stop itching. Bend has more than 30 motels and lodges, plain and fancy.

For tastes that run to luxury and bank accounts that are overloaded, there are two of the finest resorts in the Northwest, the Inn of the Seventh Mountain and the Sunriver Lodge. The latter is a vacation all by itself. The Deschutes River runs past the swimming pool, golf course, tennis courts, horseriding trails, and jogging paths. The problem is that a person may get settled into the inn or a condo and forget what there is to do in the country around.

Bend from Pilot Butte

Century Drive

For a complete list of motels and lodges write the Bend Chamber of Commerce.

Scouting Around By Car

Particularly on a first visit, scenic drives help vacationers orient themselves and inventory the attractions.

Most famous of car tours is the Cascade Lakes Highway, commonly called Century Drive—perhaps because the drive is about 100 miles long, or maybe because it goes by nearly 100 lakes. The loop, entirely on paved road, crosses the slopes of Bachelor Butte and skirts Three Sisters Wilderness, passing elegant pine forests, fish-loaded lakes, flowery meadows, and many a viewpoint and trailhead. In Bend turn west on Franklin Road, signed "Bachelor Butte, Century Drive," and once out of town make a gradual climb in 21 miles to a nameless, 6400-foot pass, then descend into headwaters of the Deschutes River and return on U.S. Highway 97 to Bend.

Forest Road 1534, unsurfaced and with limited maintenance, normally opens in early June. It diverges from Century Drive at 2 miles past Bachelor Butte, about 24 miles from Bend, passes Todd Lake in 1 mile, Three Creek Lake in 14 more miles, and at about 30 miles from Century Drive enters the town of Sisters on U.S. Highway 20. The chief glory of the drive is the wildflower color in meadows on the side of Broken Top Mountain, usually climaxing in early July. There also are close views of the rugged lava ramparts of Broken Top and long views over the lava plain. Numerous informal paths lead to higher meadows, broader views.

McKenzie Pass, open about July 1, is a longer drive, 37 miles from Bend via U.S. Highway 20 and State Highway 242. The summit, elevation 5324 feet, is a moonscape of jumbled lava sprawling miles south to North Sister Mountain and north to Mt. Washington and Three Fingered Jack. The Pacific Crest Trail winds through the black chaos. The flows look like

Broken Top Mountain from forest road No. 1534

they cooled only last week but actually are 2000 years old. (For a loop drive and good trails see "Upper Willamette Valley.")

At **Smith Rock State Park** the Crooked River meanders beneath a gaudy red wall of "painted" cliffs, 500 feet tall. Drive U.S. Highway 97 north from Bend 22 miles to Terrebonne and turn east 2 miles. Don't just look. Poke around on trails.

Bicycling

Bicycles can be rented from Bend Rental Helps, 353 S.E. Third Street, on U.S. Highway 97.

A pleasant 15-mile loop follows a 6-mile bicycle trail from town to Shevlin (city) Park, then takes a not-too-busy road to Tumalo State Park and back to Bend.

Century Drive should be the supreme trip. However, for half its distance the road is too narrow to accommodate both bicycles and unwieldy travel trailers and hulking motorhomes whose drivers are gawking at the scenery or hurrying to a fishing hole. Nevertheless, despite the perils many bikers do the whole 100 miles, stopping over to fish, swim, or camp. The route is a long, steady pull, the 21 miles from Bend to Bachelor Butte gaining 2800 feet. From there it is either a long coast back to Bend for a long day's ride or the start of a camping trip of three to five days.

Exploring the Fire

So much for orientation. It's time to tackle the vulcanism systematically. Only a few of the most dramatic features are mentioned here—for the complete menu, consult the Forest Service map-guide to Deschutes National Forest. Buy it at the Forest Supervisor's office on Revere Street in Bend or at Lava Lands Visitor Center.

Lava Butte is the mandatory start. Drive U.S. Highway 97 south 10 miles from Bend. The Forest Service's Lava Lands Visitor Center would be worth a long visit even were it in downtown Bend, offering as it does the equivalent of a college course in geology. But it happens also to provide the supreme panorama available from any road in the region. The view incredibly extends up and down the entire state of Oregon, from the Columbia River to California. North along the volcano chain are Black Butte, Three Fingered Jack, Washington, Jefferson, and finally Hood, one of the "Guardians of the Columbia." South are Thielsen, Mazama (the remnants, surrounding Crater Lake), McLoughlin, Lassen, and (maybe, when the air is especially clear) Shasta, in California. Close to the west are the Three Sisters, three separate volcanoes, plus Broken Top, Tumalo, and Bachelor Butte. Their histories cover many eons. The North and Middle Sisters and Broken Top are ancient wrecks, deeply dissected. South Sister is also old—yet active so recently it has a fresh crater in the summit containing the highest crater

Crooked River winds through Smith Rock State Park

lake in the nation. Bachelor is so new it hasn't been gouged by glaciers, is Fuji-like in contours.

Lava Butte itself, 5016 feet (rising 500 feet above the plain), is a cinder cone, a heap of lava burped out about 6000 years ago, though it has the crude look of yesterday. It is the northernmost and youngest of eight vents along the Northwest Rift Zone of Newberry Volcano. A road leads to a fire lookout cabin on the highest point of the butte.

Newberry Crater is impressive even as seen from Lava Butte, the volcanic glass shining in the sun like a field of giant mirrors. Unlike the typical Cascade stratovolcano built by many sorts of eruptions, some violent, Newberry is a Hawaii-style volcano, the result of quiet flows of very liquid lava that placidly flowed miles from the vent. Because of this the Newberry Volcano, huge though it was, never

rose more than 4000 feet above the plain. Eventually the volcano collapsed into an enormous caldera that then was divided by cinder cones into

East Lake (below) *and obsidian trail* (above) *in Newberry Crater*

Lava River Caves State Park

two depressions, now filled by Paulina and East Lakes. A massive flow of obsidian—volcanic glass—became the chief regional source of arrowheads, other tools, and ornaments. Artifacts of this glass have been found as far away as eastern Montana. Reach the Newberry area by driving U.S. Highway 97 south from Bend 40 miles. From the lakes a road climbs 4 miles to a lookout point atop Paulina Peak, at 7897 feet on the caldera rim. Look to the blue lakes and the shining glass and around the compass to four states. Then return to the lakes and walk the trails for closer looks at water and mirrors.

Hole in the Ground, 20 miles south of Newberry Crater, resembles a meteor crater but actually is an explosion crater. Forest covers the hole; a person must use a lot of imagination to visualize the blast or even to realize this is no ordinary valley.

Fort Rock is a fragment of a tuff cone built by steam explosions, then eroded by waves of the great lake that surrounded it in Pleistocene (Ice Age) times. Fort Rock is 66 miles south of Bend on State Highway 31, a long but important detour on the lava trail. A path climbs to the summit.

Lava River Caves State Park, near Lava Butte, has a mile-long lava-tube cave formed when the flow surface crusted over and still-liquid lava ran out from underneath. Lanterns can be rented for exploration.

Close-up of a tree cast, about 2½ feet in diameter, in the Lava Cast Forest

Other caves are scattered about the area, some easy to explore, others so difficult they are best left to experts.

Several caves contain ice throughout the summer. Best-known is Arnold Ice Cave, Bend's ice supply before the invention of refrigeration. The passageways that used to be cut in the ice produced beautiful formations, but now the tunnel is almost completely blocked. Best for ice formations is South Ice Cave, 1600 feet long, partly difficult. The cave locations are shown on the Forest Service map and a smaller map available from the Bend Chamber of Commerce.

Lava Cast Forest, east of Lava Butte, resulted when a flow from Newberry Volcano inundated a forest, incinerating most trees on contact but solidifying around a few before burning them and thus making the casts—the wood is gone but the shapes of the trees remain. The access road leaves U.S. Highway 97 directly oppo-

site the entrance to Sunriver. The 9 unsurfaced miles are well-marked. A ¾-mile paved trail samples the highlights. Pick up a self-guiding brochure at the trailhead.

Hiking and Climbing

The Three Sisters Wilderness in Willamette and Deschutes National Forests is the largest wildland in the Oregon Cascades, 196,708 acres—and on a fine summer weekend, nearly that many people. And, at lakes in season, more mosquitoes than mathematicians have numbers for. Nevertheless the deep forests, the meadow glades, the lakes, the wildlife, the flowers, and the views can make a hiker forget the distractions.

The standard and deservedly popular introduction is the 6-mile hike to Green Lakes. The trail starts at Sparks Lake on Century Drive, climbs gently through beautiful forest beside cold creeks, into lava flows and finally to the lake, at 6500 feet between Broken Top and South Sister. The latter is an easy ascent, safe (in good weather, after the snow melts) for any walker. This steep, boot-built path climbs through barrens of ash above trees, above dottings of flower color, to the 10,358-foot summit—and the amazing little crater lake that is ice-covered most of most summers but when it melts out is the highest-altitude swimming pool in the Cascade Range. The hike to Green Lakes can be done in a day's round trip. The climb of South Sister takes most people two days.

The Forest Service map of the Three Sisters Wilderness, at the Supervisor's office on Revere Street in Bend, shows countless other trails to lakes, lakelets, ponds, marshes, swamps, and bogs. Buy the map while picking up the wilderness permit—only available at Bend—that is required for camping. The Pacific Crest Trail passes by or near some 30-100 lakes (depending on what you call a lake) in the 40 miles north from the trailhead on Forest Service Road 2049 to the trailhead at McKenzie Pass. From the Crest Trail or trailheads along Century Drive, hikers can take any number of day trips or extended backpacks. A person who looks for it can even find solitude. And—at camps by snowfields high in rocky moraines, or in fall—freedom from mosquitoes.

The ascents of Middle Sister and North Sister involve steep snow and loose rock, requiring ice ax, rope, hard hat, and other paraphernalia of the trained climber.

South Sister and Green Lake

Cormorants roosting and nesting near Crane Prairie Reservoir

Wildlife

Some folks scarcely notice the volcanoes, busy as they are tracking the wildlife. Though elk and deer winter in the Century Drive area, they generally take to the hills by May. Smaller forest animals abound in summer but birds are the stars of the show.

During spring and summer, eagles nest near Wickiup Reservoir, grebes near Davis Lake, cormorants at Davis Lake and Crane Prairie Reservoir, and a variety of shore birds near Hosmer Lake. Near Crane Prairie are at least two great blue heron rookeries and nests of several pairs of sandhill cranes.

Top billing goes to the 60-odd pairs of ospreys that nest at Crane Prairie Reservoir and Little Lava Lake—the greatest concentration in the 48 conterminous states. The dammers of the reservoir, 50-odd years ago, had no sense of esthetics and simply let the water flood and kill a forest of lodgepole pine. The bleached snags and abundant fish have made the reservoir ideal for nesting ospreys, whose population has grown steadily. They start nesting in April but are most visible after the chicks hatch in early June, when the parents are busy chucking fish into a bunch of hungry mouths. The best viewing is from boats—along with the hundred-odd fishermen who at any one time are sharing the lake with the birds. There is an osprey nature walk with interpretive signs. However, the birds are easily spooked by people afoot (though not by people a-boat). One wonders why there is a trail at all. Boats can be rented at the resort on the east shore of the lake. While at the reservoir, look for the cormorants, at times congregated by the hundreds, even thousands. Though cormorants are not glamorous or rare and certainly not endangered, the gathering of this many is a sight and a sound not soon forgotten.

Right: *Adult osprey perched on a snag overlooking Crane Prairie Reservoir*

Bottom: *Osprey nest on a reservoir snag; Bachelor Butte in background*

rapturous about the new snow upon meeting bedraggled hikers retreating from the wilderness; one man's sport is another's misery.) There is just one catch—the summer skiers must walk up; one of the lifts is leased by a racing school, but only for students.

Even those who are totally uninterested in slipping and sliding and falling down white mountains can find fun on Bachelor—by riding a chairlift high on the volcano for grand views over a huge portion of Oregon.

Chairlifts and ski area are just off Century Drive 22 miles from Bend.

Other Interests

Deschutes County Pioneer Museum, Greenwood and Harriman Streets, is open Tuesdays and Saturdays, 1-5 p.m. Admission is free.

U.S. Forest Service Silviculture Laboratory, West 12th and Trenton, conducts field studies in forest growth. Visitors are welcome weekdays, 7:30 a.m. to 4 p.m.

U.S. Forest Service Service Center (formerly called Air Center) at Redmond is headquarters of Oregon's smoke jumpers and fire-retardant planes. Visitors welcome.

Fishing

The fighting rainbow and brown trout lurk in the Deschutes River, just waiting to snap at a juicy worm or bright fly. Lakes along Century Drive and in the wilderness are home to trout, kokanee, and silver salmon.

The 220 lakes and 235 miles of fishing streams within easy reach of Bend mean no shortage of fishing holes. Licenses and information are available at any sporting goods store. A one-day license is $2.50 for Oregon residents and visitors alike; a visitor's 10-day license is $10; a state resident's

Rental boats on Crane Prairie Reservoir

River Rafting

Three firms based in Bend, and others from California and Portland, offer float trips down the Deschutes River in summer months. In Bend contact Inn of the Seventh Mountain, Sunriver Lodge, or Sun Country Tours, Inc. (503) 389-2679. Parts of the Deschutes are even suitable for canoeing.

Summer Skiing

As long as there's a patch of white on the north slope of Bachelor Butte, there are skiers on it. Diehards keep going until mid-August—when, in some years, the first storms of winter dump a foot of fresh snow on the old. (It is not wise for skiers to get too season's license is $9. Most lake resorts rent boats and canoes, as does Bend Rental Helps.

Rock-hounding

Prineville, 35 miles northeast of Bend, claims to be the agate capital of the nation and holds an annual collectors' festival. The community owns 1000 acres, free to the public, rich in obsidian, thunder eggs, jasper, and other varieties of agate. There also are commercial agate beds where entrance is free; payment is made by the pound for anything carried out. The best-known is Richardson's Ranch, 11 miles north of Madras on U.S. 97.

Horseback Riding

Hundreds of miles of trails and thousands of square miles of open pine forest and juniper rangeland invite the rider. Horses and guide service are available at Maverick Outfitters in Redmond, headquartered at Crooked River Ranch (503) 548-7171.

Tourist Information

Bend Chamber of Commerce, 164 N.W. Hawthorne Ave., Bend, OR 97701, (503) 382-3221

Other Information

U.S. Forest Service information and maps:

Deschutes National Forest, 211 N.E. Revere St., Bend, OR 97701, (503) 382-6922

or

Lava Lands Visitor Center, Bend, OR 97701

Maps

Deschutes National Forest, 50c
Three Sisters Wilderness, 50c

Bicycle and boat rentals: Bend Rental Helps, 353 S.E. 3rd St. (on U.S. 97), Bend, OR 97701, (503) 382-2792

Reference Books

60 Hiking Trails, Central Oregon Cascades, by Don & Roberta Lowe, The Touchstone Press, P.O. Box 81, Beaverton, OR 97005

Exploring Crater Lake Country, by Ruth Kirk, University of Washington Press, 4045 Brooklyn N.E., Seattle, WA 98106

Oregon Wildlife Areas, by Bob & Ira Spring, Superior Publishing Co., P.O. Box 1710, Seattle, WA 98111

Golf Courses

Bend Golf Club (503) 382-7431, public
Sunriver Golf Club (503) 593-1221, public

KLAMATH COUNTRY

Oregon

Hub of the Wheel Vacation

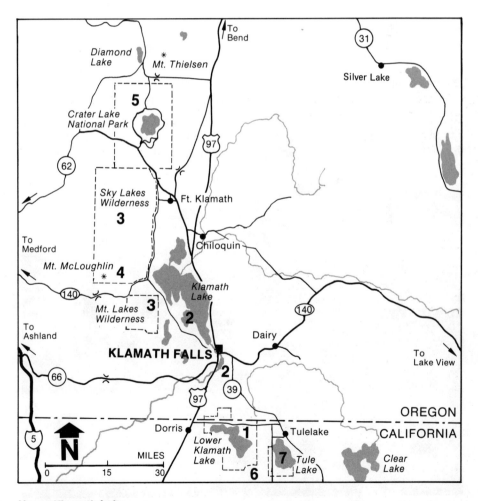

Upper Klamath Lake

Klamath Country

W hat's the biggest thing about the east-of-the Cascades, semi-desert country where Oregon and California meet? The local residents of 6600 years ago had no doubts—it was the end-of-the-world eruption of what was, until the blow-up and collapse, a huge mountain, but afterwards was a hole in the ground filled with water, Crater Lake. Waterfowl that migrate the Pacific Flyway—and birdwatchers — would say it's the lakes and marshes of the greatest wildlife refuges in the West. Some local folk —and tourists too—might vote for the Klamath County Fair.

Where to Stay

Though its population is only 20,000, Klamath Falls is the largest city in a hundred miles, trading center for 90,000 people and a major trav-elers' stopover, well-supplied with motels and hotels, swimming-pool fancy and low-rate plain, in the city, north on U.S. Highway 97, south on State Highway 39, and in Chiloquin at the north end of Upper Klamath Lake.

Resorts are located at Rocky Point on Upper Klamath Lake, Lake of the Woods, and Fish Lake. Among the guest ranches are Bar-DL Guest Ranch, P.O. Box 517, Chiloquin, OR 97624, and Take It Easy Ranch, P.O. Box 408, Fort Klamath, OR 97626, phone (503) 381-2328. Stately old Cra-ter Lake Lodge sits atop the caldera rim overlooking the lake.

On the outskirts of Klamath Falls are a KOA Campground and trailer parks. Campgrounds are found in Klamath National Forest and Cra-ter Lake National Park.

Fun and Games

Isolated by mountains and des-ert, Klamathites create their own ex-citement. In July they hold Horse and

Lake Ewauna and the city of Klamath Falls

Moore Park on Upper Klamath Lake

Buggy Days, the Shrine Circus, and a raft race. The first three weeks of August are State of Jackson Days, in memory of the time a century ago when the isolated community proposed to secede from Oregon and California and become the State of Jackson. Tourists can join the barbecue, a marathon run around the rim of Crater Lake, or a canoe race. They can watch a rodeo and a kangaroo court and attend the Governor's Ball. The climax hullaballoo of the year is the Klamath County Fair, in September when farmers of all ages, their spreads ranging from 10,000 acres to a backyard pea patch, show off crops and handicrafts. For a summer schedule write the Klamath County Chamber of Commerce.

For other fun, near Klamath Falls is a golf course. In Moore Park are six tennis courts.

History

The 1980 ashing of the Northwest by St. Helens has stimulated interest in the experience of the Clamitt (Klamath) people of 6600 years ago, who with their neighbors shared as horrid a time as any humans have survived — as some did. After all these eons the event is vividly recalled in legends.

Subsequent history of the original inhabitants is displayed at Favell Museum of Western Arts, on Main Street, which has perhaps the world's largest collection of arrowheads, other Indian artifacts, and the works of some 200 Western artists.

One of the darkest chapters in Indian history, and the most shameful in white history, is poignantly recalled in Lava Beds National Monument, scene of the Modoc War.

Klamath Falls, named Linkville when founded in 1867, no longer has falls, having exchanged them for a power reservoir on the Klamath River. The city is atop a thermal area, and in early days many buildings and homes were heated by the hot water close underground. Mineral salts tended to clog the pipes and oil, and electrical heat became cheaper, so the old sys-

tems were mostly abandoned but are now being revived —this is one city that won't get cold when the Arabs turn off the spigot for good.

Nothing as interesting as the Modoc War has happened since then, but there's much of interest at the Klamath County Museum on Main Street. Another Main Street museum is in the four-story Baldwin Building, built in 1906, formerly a hardware store, then a hotel; for information on visiting hours inquire at the County Museum. At Collier State Park, 30 miles north of Klamath Falls on U.S. Highway 97, is the Logging Museum with early logging equipment, including a huge steam locomotive that didn't run on railroad tracks but on roads, dragging logs to the mill.

Wildlife

During migrations of fall and spring millions of waterfowl of a score of species pause in Klamath Basin to rest and feed before continuing journeys south or north. At any one time more than 500,000 are assembled, and when as few as a tenth of these pass overhead, the sky seems alive with wings.

In the dead of winter the stars are 500 bald eagles, down from the frozen north to take the waters—and the waterfowl crippled by hunters and left to die.

Summer is quieter but not less fascinating because that is family time, when one can watch a mother duck followed by a dozen little balls of fluff, or young eyes peeking out from

Top to bottom: *Western grebe and baby, white pelicans, and an American coot on Lower Klamath Lake. Right: Snow geese over Tule Lake*

under the wing of a mother grebe. And then there are the white pelicans, birds so big and awkward-looking they obviously can't fly—but they do, and gracefully. When they stretch out their black-tipped wings to full 9-foot span, they appear to soar effortlessly.

The best summer birdwatching is at Lower Klamath Lake and Tule Lake National Wildlife Refuges. Drive south 17 miles from Klamath Falls on U.S. Highway 97. Within a mile after entering California, turn east on California State Highway 161, skirting the Lower Klamath Refuge. Find the entrance and take the "short tour," then drive on towards Tulelake and follow signs to the refuge. At the headquarters get maps and a bird list and follow marked tour routes. The white pelicans are everywhere in the basin, but the best chances of sighting are on Lake Ewauna, inside the city limits of Klamath Falls, and on the two tour routes here noted.

Hiking and Climbing

The Pacific Crest Trail runs the length of the Cascade Crest and is usually snow-free by early July. It passes through the Sky Lakes (proposed) Wilderness, a chain of alpine lakes, and connects to trails to Mountain Lakes Wilderness, with more lakes and peaks.

Broad views from naked lava slopes above timberline are the feature of 9495-foot Mt. McLoughlin, whose summit, formerly site of a fire lookout, has a 6-mile trail to the top. The snow stays on upper reaches until August.

All these trailheads are reached from State Highway 140 near Lake of the Woods. However, the best way to Seven Lakes Basin, one of the prettiest parts of the Sky Lakes, is via Forest Service Road 232 near Fort Klamath; a U.S. Forest Service map is needed to navigate the forest roads—get one at Forest Service headquarters on the west side of Klamath Falls or at the

North side of Mt. Shasta, Shastina on right

Phantom Ship Rock and Crater Lake

office in the Post Office Building.

Other hiking is described in sections on Crater Lake National Park and Lava Beds National Monument.

The only real climbing in the area is on 14,162-foot Mt. Shasta, 70 miles to the south on U.S. Highway 97. The south slopes are an easy walk for anyone experienced in snow travel and able to breathe and walk at that elevation without getting sick. The north side of the huge volcano has the largest glaciers in California. High Chalet, 737 Main Street in Klamath Falls, (503) 884-3283, offers several seminars there a year, three-day schools on basic mountaineering with emphasis on ice, concluding with a climb to the summit. High Chalet also leads climbs on the south side of the mountain.

Crater Lake National Park

One of the oldest and most famous national parks, Crater Lake has beauties to dazzle the most jaded connoisseur of Western scenery. Post card photographs may seem banal— until one has been there on the caldera rim at sunset and seen the lava slopes turn from gold to purple, and the water from blue to black, or at sunrise and seen the color procession in reverse.

The drama of the lake's creation is as awesome as the beauty, and never more so than since 1980, when a little neighbor of Mazama's to the north echoed the 42 times more horrendous explosion of 6600 years ago.

From Klamath Falls drive 46 miles to the park via U.S. Highway 97, State Highway 62, and then to the caldera rim. At the visitor center learn how the volcano grew, blew, and collapsed and how the hole filled with snow water. Finally, complete the 33-mile around-the-lake rim drive, stopping often to examine rocks polished and scratched by the glaciers that once flowed from high above, where now is only sky.

Lake of the Woods and Mt. McLoughlin

Leave the car and walk. Take the short path to the lookout on The Watchman. Descend the Cleetwood Trail to the shore and ride the tour boat past the Phantom Ship to Wizard Island. Ascend the 2½-mile trail to the top of Mt. Scott, 8926 feet, highest remnant of old Mazama and offering an arm's-length perspective on the lake. Everywhere admire wildflowers struggling on barren lava.

Fishing

I've learned to be skeptical about chamber of commerce claims that fishing is great; catching is believing. However, Klamath County has plenty of lakes and streams, though there is some question whether the fish really leap in your boat before you even cast your line. Boats can be rented at Rocky Point Resort on Upper Klamath Lake and the resorts on Lake of the Woods and Fish Lake. Stream fishing is said to be good in Williamson River near Klamath Marsh, 45 miles north of Klamath Falls on U.S. Highway 97.

Canoeing

Crystal Creek and Recreation Creek, on the west side of Upper Klamath Lake, and Lake Ewauna in the city of Klamath Falls, are excellent for paddling. The middle of Upper Klamath Lake is not recommended —fierce winds rise without warning and set the shallow waters chopping with whitecaps.

Canoes can be rented from Rocky Point Resort on the west side of Upper Klamath Lake.

Lava Beds National Monument

Except in early summer when the desert is a glory of flowers in bloom, the above-ground scenery is grim—a vastness of raw lava only a few thousand years old, meagerly sprinkled with sagebrush and clumps of gnarled junipers. The below-ground scenery, though, is something else. Within the lava flows are innumerable caves formed when the surface cooled and crusted over and still-liquid lava ran out from under. To date 300 lava tubes have been found in the monument. The best have trails down inside, usually with entry stairways or ladders where needed. The average visitor can get all the caving wanted on the loop trail at the headquarters, where the Park Service will loan you a large lantern ideal for the tour. The loop passes enough caves to keep you busy a full day—and a wondrous day it is, alternately baking in the desert sun, then chilling in the ever-cold darkness— baking and chilling, baking and chilling, as the eyes alternately adjust to stygian night, then blinding day, back and forth. The campground at the headquarters is a comfortable base for exploration.

There's much more to see on or near roads of the monument, many other trails leading to caves and cinder cones. On roads and trails, watch for deer. Behind the fence that encloses them in a protected pasture, watch for bighorn sheep. The species was exterminated hereabouts by early settlers but the Park Service is raising a herd that eventually will be released in the lava wilds.

Also on roads and trails are battlegrounds and camps of the Modoc War, which ended in 1872 with the exile of the Modocs to the Indian Territories and the theft of their last lands by settlers. But before that happened, "Captain Jack" and a band of a few dozen men, women, and children holed up in lava "forts" and stood off the U.S. Army for six months. When we were at headquarters a history lecture was delivered by a young woman, a National Park Service ranger, whose grandfather was one of the Modocs lynched by the whites. She passed around history books written by the

A stronghold of Captain Jack, Lava Beds National Monument

settlers, describing her people as murderers and renegades and idolizing the settlers as "Indian fighters." She said that her people knew the settlers as criminals and honored the memory of Captain Jack and companions as "white fighters." They didn't speak of a "Modoc War" but of a "Homesteader War."

Tourist Information

Klamath County Chamber of Commerce, 125 N. 8th St., Klamath Falls, OR 97601, (503) 884-5193

Other Information

U.S. Forest Service information and maps:

Winema National Forest, P.O. Bldg. (P.O. Box 1390), Klamath Falls, OR 97601, (503) 882-7761

Maps:

Winema National Forest, 50c
Mountain Lakes Wilderness, 50c

Reference Books

Exploring Crater Lake Country, by Ruth Kirk, University of Washington Press, 4045 Brooklyn N.E., Seattle, WA 98106

Oregon Wildlife Areas, by Bob & Ira Spring, Superior Publishing Co., P.O. Box 1710, Seattle, WA 98111

Golf Course

Klamath Falls, Reames Golf & Country Club, 18 holes, private

NORTHEAST OREGON

Oregon

Rolling Wheel Vacation

Ride the Snake River through Hells Canyon, deepest gorge in the nation. Hike meadows of the Wallowa Mountains, largest alpine area in Oregon. Fish, prowl ghost towns, loll around a dude ranch, join the whoop-dee-doo of the Pendleton Round-Up, the West's wildest and woolliest rodeo and Indian show that draws visitors in droves.

The vacation is a loop tour that can start anywhere, such as Bend on U.S. Highway 26 or Baker on Interstate 84. We picked it up at Arlington, on Interstate 84 about 140 miles east of Portland, so that's the way the trip is described here.

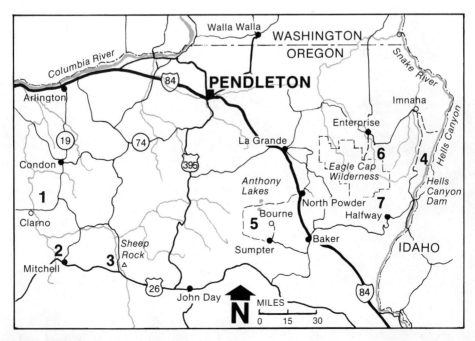

Hells Canyon

John Day Fossil Beds National Monument

From Arlington drive State Highway 19 south 60 miles to Fossil. In late July and August see farmers harvesting grain, giant combines often working near the road, and mobs of grouse, chukar, and quail feeding on grain spilt by trucks. In Fossil visit the county courthouse, built in 1910.

Base your exploration on the fossils, some of them 70 million years old, and the gaudy rocks and dramatic cliffs, at a plain motel in a small town or a fancy one in John Day, or a campground operated commercially or by state parks—there are no housing or campgrounds in the monument. The monument consists of three units, widely scattered. Whichever you come to first, be sure to pick up the free National Park Service brochure and map which shows all the units.

Clarno Unit. Located 20 miles north of Fossil on State Highway 218, this unit contains some of the oldest fossils ever found, as well as towering palisades of brown-to-bronze rock.

Painted Hills Unit. Reached from Mitchell on U.S. Highway 26, the Painted Hills are banded with bright red, brown, and yellow earth.

Sheep Rock Unit. Named for the dominant peak of the area, this unit has the Visitors Center, in a farmhouse on a working ranch. Geological formations are described and fossils displayed. This unit is located near the junction of U.S. Highway 26 and State Highway 19.

For this next part of the tour, from Sheep Rock drive Highway 26 to John Day (good motels) and on to Unity Lake, then turn north on State Highway 7 to Baker (good motels).

Painted Hills, John Day National Monument

Old mining town of Bourne   *Anthony Lake*

Elkhorn Mountains

Rich in mining history, with two well-preserved ghost towns, the Elkhorn Mountains also have small but lovely lakes and uncrowded trails. Ask at the U.S. Forest Service Ranger Station in Baker (or write—Baker, OR 97814) for the brochure, *The Elkhorn Drive,* describing a 105-mile auto tour on roads partly paved, partly gravel. Highlights are Phillips Lake (reservoir), a ride on the Sumpter Valley Railroad, a restored narrow-gauge railroad with a wood-burning locomotive, and the ghost towns of Sumpter and Bourne, both with a few buildings left. Miles of river bottom in the area are devastated; see remains of the monster gold dredge that enriched a few miners and ruined a beautiful valley. The tour climbs past the site of Granite and the Cougar-Independence Mines to Anthony Lakes; there, hike the ½-mile Trail of the Alpine Glacier. Back at Baker visit the United States Mountain Bank to view the display of gold nuggets from the region, including one weighing 80 ounces.

Wallowa Mountain Loop and Hat Point

A highway loop of 250 miles encircles the Eagle Cap Wilderness of the Wallowa Mountains. Sidetrips lead to breathtaking Wallowa Lake, a stunning look down from Hat Point into Hells Canyon, and Hells Canyon Dam. Along the way are valley-bottom farms, rolling sagebrush, prairies, forested hills, and rivers winding through little canyons.

Drive State Highway 82 from LaGrande through Enterprise to Joseph. Sidetrip 6 miles to Wallowa Lake, dammed by moraines of the glacier that issued from the impressive fault scarp of the Wallowa Mountains and sprawled over the plain.

Next drive paved road to Imnaha and the start of one of the most incredible auto tours in the Northwest, 24 miles to Hat Point, tortuously and steeply climbing a high ridge, then following the crest. Allow two to three hours each way—which says something about the cruel road and its surface of dirt, mud, and sharp chunks of

Wallowa Lake

lava rock. If your car is a street machine with little clearance, forget it. With any car, going and coming in a single day is hard labor, no fun. Instead stay overnight at the Hat Point Campground—a plan that offers the bonus of watching sunset on peaks of the Seven Devils and miles of ridges and canyons, the largest wildland in the Northwest, and looking down down *down* to night in Hells Canyon and a solitary light twinkling at a ranch by the Snake River. Do the trip in early July, as soon as the mud is pretty well dried up, for what may be the grandest flower show in the Northwest, starting with dry-land plants at Imnaha and climbing to alpine meadows that blend species common to the Cascades with species common to the Rockies, all in one dazzling color riot.

Back at Imnaha, drive the road, partly paved, partly gravel, 62 miles to State Highway 86 near Oxbow Dam. Sidetrip 30 miles to Hells Canyon for the Snake River trips, then return to Baker and LaGrande.

Eagle Cap Wilderness

Parts of the Wallowa Mountains remind a hiker of the east slopes of the Cascades, others of the Montana Rockies, and still others of the High Sierra. With peaks rising to 10,000 feet, lakes in glacier-scooped cirques, and forests that open into parklands and meadows at about 7000-8000 feet, the Eagle Cap Wilderness is the largest protected wilderness in Oregon and, despite the distance from population centers, in part as crowded as any. The advice of experts is to shun the lakes, full of fish and full-up with fishermen and other campers. Do so and you can have 1930s-type solitude for a week-long backpack, and flowers, flowers, flowers.

Despite the crowds, you may wish to sample the classic north-side approach, via Wallowa Lake. Obtain your wilderness permit at the trailhead ranger tent and climb 3800 feet in 12 miles to 8500-foot Glacier Lake.

For a popular south-side entry, drive from Halfway to the semi-ghost town of Cornucopia and walk a jeep trail 2 miles to Queen Mine and the Pine Lake trailhead, 5200 feet. Climb 6 miles to the lake at 7600 feet, surrounded by rocks and flowers.

The horse rider can take guided day trips from Wallowa Lake or Cornucopia. For longer trips contact a packer. For list of packers, write Forest Supervisor, Wallowa-Whitman National Forest, P.O. Box 907, Baker, OR 97814.

Glacier Lake, Eagle Cap Wilderness

Hells Canyon National Recreation Area

Here is the deepest hole in the United States, even deeper than the Grand Canyon. The Snake River flowing through its miles of wilderness is one of the most exciting white-water trips in the West. Indians traversed the canyon from prehistoric times, and many of their pictographs can be seen. Settlers homesteaded wherever a flat bench let them build a house and run a few cows. For years a powerboat from Lewiston carried mail and cargo part way upriver to the ranchers; though a few ranches remain, the boats now mostly carry tourists.

The closest motels are at Payette and Weiser in Idaho and Baker and LaGrande in Oregon. Along the reservoirs above Hells Canyon and Oxbow Dams are campgrounds of Idaho Power Company. Nearby are many National Forest and commercial campgrounds, including Radium Hot Springs at Haines, with a hot pool to soak in. (Some of these accommodations also serve as bases for the Elkhorn and Wallowa Mountains, following on the tour.)

All river trips start from road's end at Hells Canyon Dam, 23 miles downriver from Oxbow. The jet boat operated by Hells Canyon Navigation Company leaves four times daily for two-hour cruises. No reservations are needed, you get a good sample of the canyon, and the captain relates a running commentary on history and geology.

Guided Float trip in Hells Canyon

The ultimate experience is a raft or dory trip through Hells Canyon, floating 32 miles to Pittsburg Landing or 79 miles to the mouth of the Grande Ronde River. The number of people on the river at any one time is controlled, so reservations must be made far in advance. Those wishing to do the trip on their own, on their own craft, should reserve time six months ahead; write U.S. Forest Service, Pine Ranger District, Halfway, OR 97834: The Forest Service maintains a list of the more than two dozen outfitters licensed to take guests; again, reservations are required. These firms offer trips of varying length, depending on how much time is allowed for exploring. Hells Canyon Navigation offers a one-day float trip to Pittsburg Landing, with the return by airplane the same afternoon. However, their recommended float is six days, the usual duration of the guided trips.

Baker's Bar M Ranch

For something completely different try this guest ranch on the old Pendleton-LaGrande stagecoach trail. The main building, a log hotel built in 1864 as a stagecoach stop and hot springs resort, still is used as a dining room, and the springs still heat a large swimming pool. Horses and guides are provided for day or overnight rides in the adjacent National Forest. For a brochure write the ranch at Route 1, Adams, OR 97810 or call (503) 566-3381. Space is very limited and reservations are essential.

Pendleton Round-Up

Started in 1910 by local ranchers, the Round-Up is staged the second week of September, featuring stagecoach races, one of the greatest gatherings of Indians in the West, and the standard rodeo events. Motels are booked full months ahead, but by use of private homes the Chamber of Commerce sees to it that everyone has a roof and a bed.

Baker's Bar M Ranch near Pendleton

Hand-hewn logs on the old stagecoach building, at Baker's Bar M Ranch

Tourist Information:

Baker Chamber of Commerce, 490 Campbell St., P.O. Box 69, Baker, OR 97814, (503) 523-5855

LaGrande Chamber of Commerce, 101 Depot, P.O. Box 308, LaGrande, OR 97850, (503) 963-8588

Pendleton Chamber of Commerce, 37 S.E. Dorion, P.O. Box 1446, Pendleton, OR 97801, (503) 276-7411

Other Information

U.S. Forest Service information and maps:

Wallowa-Whitman National Forest, Federal Office Bldg. (P.O. Box 907), Baker, OR 97814, (503) 523-6391

Maps

Wallowa-Whitman National Forest North Half, 50c
Wallowa-Whitman National Forest South Half, 50c
Eagle Cap Wilderness, 50c

Brochure

"The Elkhorn Drive," free in 1980

River permits:

U.S. Forest Service, Pine Ranger District, Halfway, OR 97834

Golf Courses

Baker, Baker Golf Course, 9 holes, public
LaGrande, LaGrande Country Club, 9 holes, private
Pendleton, Pendleton Golf & Country Club, 9 holes, private

HIGH EASTERN DESERT

Oregon-Idaho

Rolling Wheel Vacation

Everybody loves the desert in late afternoon, when shadows are long and the land is richly colored in reds and purples. But what about the rest of the day, when the furnace sun blazes on horizons of fried sagebrush? This is not a vacation for everyone—in fact, it's hardly for anyone, and certainly not for a family with small children. There are miles and miles of lonesome roads and ghost towns, abundant wildlife, rugged mountains, and flower fields. But there are no cool forests, no lakes for swimming, very few streams, and sun, sun, and sun, and dust, dust, and dust. Yet after every visit, and every vow of "never again," we find ourselves wanting to go back. Truly, the high desert is among the grand experiences on earth—grandest, maybe, in short

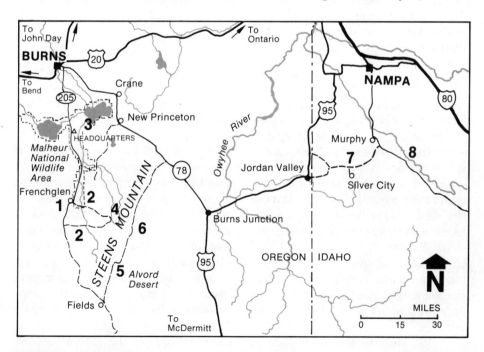

East side of Steens Mountain

White pelicans at Malheur National Wildlife Refuge

doses. Those with a taste for a visit of more than several days should get the guidebook, *Oregon's Great Basin Country,* which describes weeks of fascinating explorations, and the map of Steens Mountain, available from the Bureau of Land Management in Burns.

The Best Time—There is none.

Spring and fall are the seasons for migratory birds, and in spring they are in courtship plumage. Spring is cooler than summer, if still hot. And in spring the desert bursts out in a brief explosion of color as the wildflowers bloom a few days, then wither. But the timing is unpredictable, and we've never been lucky enough to see the big show. But we have seen and heard black clouds of mosquitoes. And because the roads were still blocked by the snow that doesn't melt off until July, we couldn't get up Steens Mountain.

So, despite the heat, I guess we've enjoyed summer trips most. The flowers are blooming on Steens, which then is accessible by car. The birds are less brilliant, but the mature ones are trailing flocks of little babies.

Where to Stay—There aren't many.

There aren't many choices.

If a roof is wanted, there are good motels in Burns, basic ones at Jordan Valley, and a small rustic inn at Frenchglen, and that's it. The little Frenchglen Hotel is worth a stop for a meal—food is served family style in quantities suited to the appetite of a hard-working cowboy. The hotel is small, so if planning to stay overnight (or even for dinner), call ahead for reservations (503) 493-2565. The roads are unsuitable for trailers or large recreational vehicles. The best bet is to carry water and sunshades, stock up on groceries at Burns, the last good chance, and stay at primitive campgrounds at Page Spring, 3 miles from Frenchglen, Fish Lake and Blitzen Campground on the side of Steens Mountain, and Silver City.

Malheur National Wildlife Refuge

From Burns drive State Highway 78, signed "Crane and New Princeton," about 2 miles and turn south on State Highway 206, signed "Frenchglen." After 28 miles turn right and follow signs to the refuge headquarters. (A longer, more interesting way includes visits to Malheur Cave, Crane Hot Springs, the famous Round Barn, Diamond Crater with its fresh-looking lava, and the start of the Desert Trail planned ultimately to go all the way to Mexico. See *Oregon's Great Basin Country.*)

Porcupine, weasel, deer, and antelope live here in one of the nation's most important wildlife refuges, but mainly birds. During fall and winter migrations the clouds of waterfowl darken the sky. Summer is also busy, eggs being hatched and families raised. The wide variety of habitats supports a wide variety of species. Most notable are the 200 nesting pairs of sandhill cranes, huge birds with long legs, 90-inch wing spans, and bright red caps. White pelicans, Canada geese, egrets, and swans are good watching—none more fun than a mama duck followed by a dozen fluffy babes.

Begin by stopping at headquarters for a map of the refuge and an auto tour brochure. Follow the center patrol road, well-graveled, up Donner and Blitzen Valley 38 miles to Frenchglen. We've driven the route five different occasions. We like late spring best because the birds are in courting plumage. However, one trip in mid-August we saw two huge flocks of white pelicans, some egrets, great blue herons, 100 or more sandhill cranes, and several broods of ducks. Our most memorable encounter came in the middle of the road. A weasel was chasing a covey of quail, a dozen or more of the tiniest chicks we'd ever seen, and mother and father were dashing back and forth so madly it was hard to know who was chasing whom. Abruptly the weasel vanished—either frightened by our car, or worn out by the chase, or with a mouthful of chick. It all happened too fast to tell.

American bittern (top) *and sandhill cranes* (bottom), *from a refuge road*

Steens Mountain

The west slope of this giant fault block is so gentle it is hard to comprehend the hugeness of the mountain; the listed elevation of 9733 feet seems impossible until, even in August, patches of snow are seen. Viewing from the east, one doesn't question the height because the abrupt fault scrap is all cliffs and buttresses. The mountain has another surprise unguessed from afar—four deep gorges gouged by glaciers 10,000 years ago. The hiking is spectacular, but a person has to keep in mind that though the mountain is surrounded by hot desert, snow can fall on the heights any day of summer.

Two roads climb the west side from Frenchglen. Snow usually blocks them until July, and autos are not allowed until the mud dries. Road conditions vary from year to year. When open, they usually are in good shape to Fish Lake and Blitzen Campground. Before attempting to go higher, check with the BLM office in Burns; often the higher reaches are too rocky for ordinary passenger cars. But they can always be walked.

In season—normally, middle July to early August—the ridges of Steens are a mass of wildflowers. On a background of bright-yellow balsam root are splashes and dots of phlox, shooting star, bitterroot, miner's lettuce, snow buttercup, steershead bleeding heart, stonecrop, cinquefoil, violet, primrose, waterleaf, yellow bells, and alpine lily. There also are such rare plants as moss gentian *(Gentiana prostrata)*, one-flowered gentian *(G. simplex)*, dwarf skullcap *(Scutellaria nana)*, white penstemon *(Penstemon pratensis)*, Sierra onion *(Allium campanulatum)*, and early coral root *(Corallorhiza trifida)*.

Alvord Desert

For a few the 200-mile loop around Steens Mountain is a desert gourmet's delight—a primitive area with an annual rainfall of 4 to 6 inches, miles of sagebrush, hot springs, a vast dry lake with a bed of baked clay, and maybe one house every 5 to 10 miles. For others it's a hot, dusty, monotonous, endless drive. No accommodations, no formal campgrounds. Just sagebrush, jackrabbits, dust, sun. Think things over before setting out;

Deserted store near Alvord Lake

Wagon wheel at a farm in Field

Hot springs near borax quarry

even a gourmet can get hot and pooped. From Frenchglen to State Highway 78 are 150 miles of dirt road. Gas can be bought at Frenchglen and 51 miles farther on at Fields. Repairs? Well, if the car breaks, it may never get home. In true pioneer spirit, the first rancher along will stop and help but it might be an hour or two.

The road switchbacks up a steep hill from Frenchglen and heads south. The first 15 miles are paved, the rest is well-graded gravel. The way rounds the west side of Steens Mountain and at 50 miles reaches a junction. A mile south is Field, consisting of a gas pump, small store, and restaurant; turn north instead.

In about 3 miles spot a primitive road on the right and drive (rough but generally possible) 2½ miles, then walk a final ¼ mile to an abandoned borax quarry. Search around for the large pool of warm water, nearby hot springs, and a ground surface of crusty

Hot spring bath

Alvord Desert, approximately 50 square miles of caked mud

borax that sounds hollow when you walk on it. The easiest time to find the hot springs is early morning when they steam in the cool air.

Resuming the journey north, pass Alvord Lake, ordinarily dry by mid-July, several ranches, and climb over a slight rise to a grand view of Alvord Desert—more than 7 miles wide and 9 miles long. At first glance it seems a muddy lake, and in winter the desert indeed is covered by an inch or two of water. By summer what you're seeing is very flat, sun-baked mud.

The road descends. Spot a primitive road dropping to the desert edge. Unless there has been recent rain (very unlikely in summer), you can drive anywhere on the enormous flat. You'll see tracks of ranchers who regularly cross to reach various holdings.

In a couple miles more on the main road see a small parking area. A hundred feet away are two pools, one hot and the other very hot. Local ranchers have built a small dressing room and take regular dips in the pools. One grizzled fellow told us it sure is wonderful in winter—you step out of the hot pool with a warm glow and for a few minutes don't even know the air temperature is 10 degrees below.

The way goes north another 40 miles to State Highway 78, the monotony relieved by ever-changing perspectives on Steens Mountain, some inaccessible lakes that often are dry, an occasional ranch, and not much else. Turn east 26 miles on Highway 78 to Burns Junction through country whose only redeeming feature is the speed you can make on the pavement.

Idaho Hotel (above) **and a private house built in the 1860s** (below), *in Silver City*

Silver City

High in the mountains just over the border in Idaho, in 1860s Silver City was a bustling metropolis. It never became a full ghost, always has had a few inhabitants, and therefore has many buildings still standing.

From Burns Junction drive U.S. Highway 95 to Jordan Valley and follow signs to DeLamar Silver Mine. The road is paved a few miles. Be careful at a Y in about 4 miles to take the correct fork. From pavement end the gravel road is wide and well-graded, climbing steadily to a ridge, then going on the crest for miles, with views to modern surface mining. At 17 miles from Jordan Valley is the end of good road at the DeLamar Mining operation.

The next 9 miles along the old stagecoach trail are very interesting —which means slow. In places the way follows ruts of the wagons, and you may wonder if the road wasn't in better shape then, when stagecoaches ran daily. Mines, cabins, and rusting equipment of the 19th century are passed, and workings of 1980s prospectors, ever hopeful they'll find something a century of diggers missed. Allow about 30-45 minutes to cover this last stretch (about the same speed as a stagecoach) to Silver City, elevation 6179 feet, amid 8000-foot rolling hills. The streets are as rough as the wagon road. There is a small campground here but no other accommodations.

The Silver City Hotel sags a bit and the porch railings are gone, but meals are served and the lobby looks ready to welcome guests from the stagecoach—the furniture looks as if it did. The two-story schoolhouse now is a museum with pictures and artifacts of the city and mines. It's a pleasure simply to walk the streets and study the buildings, all privately owned. A few are open to the public, and a donation helps defray costs of maintenance, as does a small entrance fee at the museum.

From Silver City the stagecoach road climbs east over a 6500-foot pass to a spectacular view 4000 feet down to farms by the Snake River. The road is dirt but fairly decent, dropping in 20 miles to Idaho State Highway 78 a few miles south of Murphy and a gas station.

Snake River Birds of Prey Natural Area

You are now amid one of the greatest known concentrations (600 pairs) of nesting raptors (hawks, bald eagles, and peregrine falcons). To see them, though, even from a distance, you'll need help because some roads are closed in nesting season. To gain a general notion of the area and possibly sight soaring birds, drive south 25 miles on Highway 78 to Grand View, turn onto Idaho State Highway 67, and view the Snake River from approaches to the bridge.

The best birding is on a three-day float trip down the Snake with Mackay Bar guides (for information contact Mountain Hosts, Inc., 411 Main St., Ketchum, Idaho 83340, phone 208 726-7471). The trips are expensive because they include professional guides, expert naturalists, and fantastic meals.

Tourist Information

Harney County Junior Chamber of Commerce, 18 West D Street, Burns, OR 97720, (503) 573-2636

Other Information

Bureau of Land Management information and map:
   Bureau of Land Management, Burns, OR 97720

Map

Steens Mountain, free in 1980

Reference Books

Oregon's Great Basin Country, by Denzel & Nancy Ferguson, Gail Graphics, Burns, OR 97720

Hiking the Oregon High Desert, by Bruce Hayse, distributed by Oregon High Desert Study Group, P.O. Box 25, St. Paul, OR 97137

Oregon Wildlife Areas, by Bob & Ira Spring, Superior Publishing Co., P.O. Box 1710, Seattle, WA 98111

INDEX